BABY
GOT
FACTS
TOTALLY
'90s
TRIVIA

BUZZY COHEN

PUZZLE
WRIGHT
PRESS
New York

I'd like to dedicate this to my parents, Amy and Marvin Cohen, my wife Elisha, Alex Trebek, and of course Pee-Wee Herman.

ISBN 978-1-4549-5393-7

For information about custom editions, special sales, and premium purchases, please contact specialsales@unionsquareandco.com.

Printed in Canada

2 4 6 8 10 9 7 5 3 1

unionsquareandco.com

Cover design by Erik Jacobsen
Cover illustration by Stanley Chow
Interior image credits: TeddyandMia/Shutterstock.com (pp. 56–57), PeterHermesFurian/iStock/Getty Images Plus (p. 76, 120); Sterling Publishing Co., Inc. (p. 80)

CONTENTS

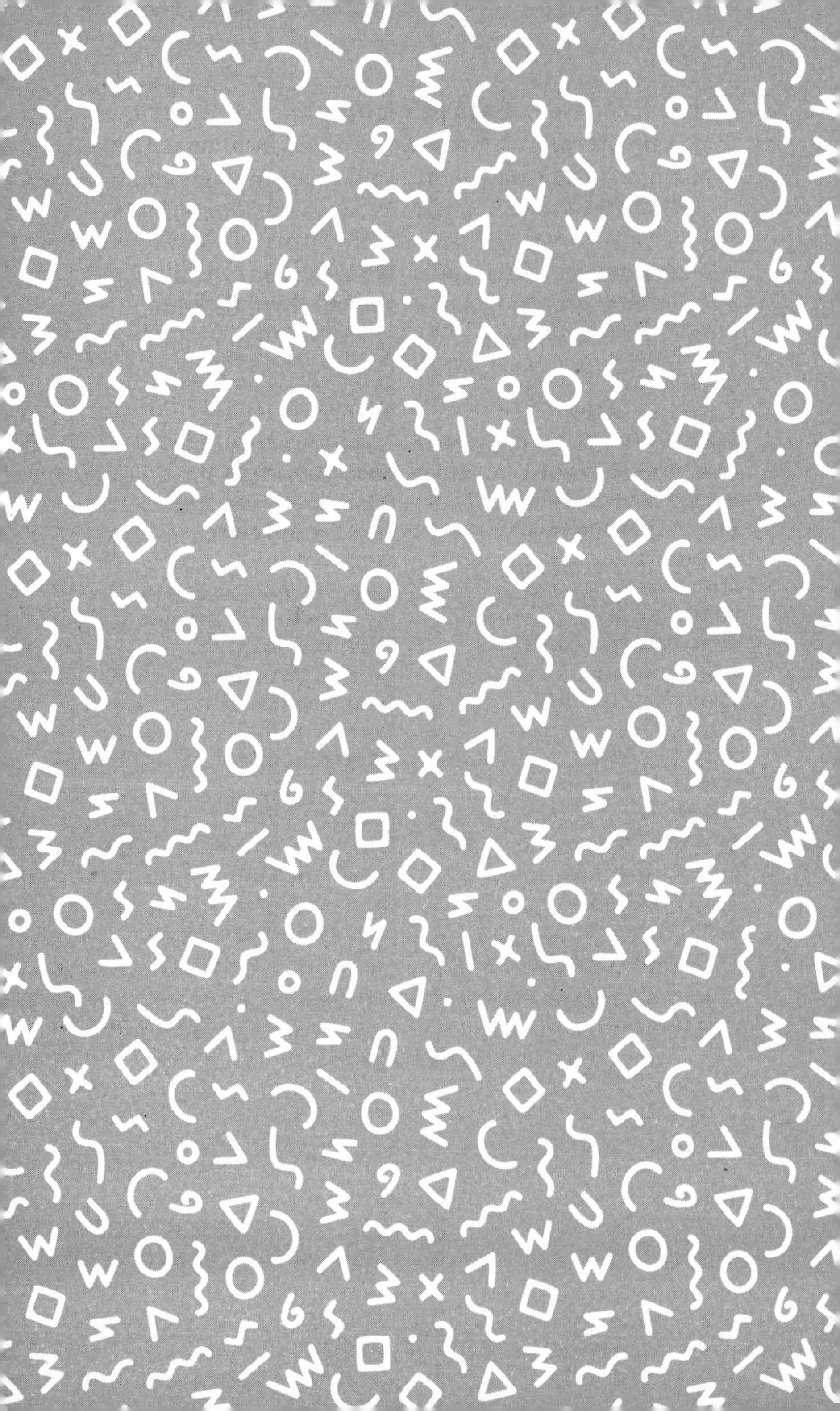

Introduction

I remember spending many Friday nights as a youth watching the 1993 film *Dazed and Confused* in my parents basement (it was one of the four films we owned on VHS). My friends and I would eat pizza on pleather couches that sat atop wall-to-wall leopard-print carpet (my mom figured out that when you spilled soda on leopard print it didn't show as much).

There's a line in the film where the nerdy characters of Mike, Tony, and Cynthia are hanging around discussing their disdain for the era in which they're living. Cynthia is hopeful for the future, sharing her reasoning: "It's like the 'every other decade' theory, you know? The '50s were boring. The '60s rocked. The '70s, oh my god, they obviously suck. Maybe the '80s will be ... radical."

I'm sure filmmaker Richard Linklater knew when he wrote that line that those of us watching 17 years after the Bicentennial would be thinking, "Man, the '70s were so freaking cool, not like the crappy '90s we're in now." Well, past is prologue, and the current wave of '90s nostalgia was as inevitable as the ones that gave us *Grease*, *Happy Days*, the Stray Cats, *The Wonder Years*, and, later, *That '70s Show*. If *Dazed and Confused* was remade in 2024, it would be set in 1997, with a bunch of teens driving around in Acura Integras and Honda CR-Vs listening to "Bitter Sweet Symphony" and "Barbie Girl," looking for a party. But for millennials like myself, this is our first time having a period we actually lived through come back into vogue, and there is something surprising and unsettling about it—something worth investigating.

I am very much a child of the '90s; I was born in 1985 and spent my formative years in New Jersey. At first I thought New Jersey was the most '90s state, but I've since decided it's Illinois. *Home Alone*, Lollapalooza, *Family Matters*, *ER*, Michael Jordan's Chicago Bulls, and *Wayne's World* all stick out as touchpoints of '90s culture—and it makes sense perhaps that a midwestern state was a home to so much '90s culture, since the '90s were a deeply transitional moment. The fall of the USSR, the rise of the Internet, the launch of Fox News and Napster—it all happened in a tight 10 years that also gave us deeply disparate music trends (grunge *and* Britney Spears?!), as well as a growing sense of global culture.

I was of course unaware of this. I was just living my suburban life, coming home from school, putting on cartoons, popping some Spaghetti-O's in the microwave, washing 'em down with a peach Snapple Iced Tea, and then having some Dunkaroos (if I was lucky!) for dessert. My older sister made sure I kept up with culture, though, occasionally making me watch shows I wasn't interested in (*90210*, *Melrose Place*, and *My So-Called Life*, to name a few), and also introducing me to bands she thought I'd like. After attending an Alanis Morissette concert, she gave me a T-shirt and CD of the opening band, who she thought I'd love: none other than Radiohead.

My love for trivia was born in the '90s as well. *Jeopardy!* had established itself as a staple of the American game show diet after being rebooted in syndication in 1984. Some folks liked *Wheel of Fortune* or *The Price Is Right*, but for me it was always about *Jeopardy!* I will admit that I also loved *Supermarket Sweep*, but maybe it was hearing Johnny Gilbert, longtime *Jeopardy!* announcer, giving play-by-plays of people crashing their shopping carts into crates of turkeys that made the grocery-based action click for my pre-adolescent brain. Every night my family's TV was tuned to ABC7 to enjoy a mustachioed Alex Trebek leading us through 61 answers and questions on everything from Opera and Bodies of Water to Pop Music and Wordplay. My viewing habits were so consistent that I could even "feel" how long the commercial breaks were. I'd switch over to the local Fox affiliate for a few moments of a syndicated *Simpsons* rerun, and always switch back to *Jeopardy!* as it was returning from commercial break, never missing one clue.

My trivia mind was not limited to TV quiz shows, though. In the pre-tablet era, family road trips required a different strategy. A GameBoy could maybe keep a kid occupied for a bit, but the battery life on those things was not enough for the kind of long-hauls I remember doing. My mom discovered the Brain Quest quiz cards and I would churn through those as the miles rolled by in our family Lincoln.

The end of the '90s saw a big shift in mainstream trivia: *Who Wants to Be A Millionaire* launched on ABC in August of 1999, and suddenly quiz shows went from a syndicated diversion to a prime-time television event. While *Millionaire* has left the airwaves, it is undoubtedly responsible for the fact that trivia nerds can now become household names.

My love for facts never ebbed, though my only outlet for it for many years was shouting answers at the TV (and, later, at the moderator of my high school quiz bowl games). It wasn't until I appeared on *Jeopardy!* in 2016 that the wide world of trivia reopened to me, leading me eventually to this tome before you.

When I started working on this book of trivia, I imagined I'd hit all the well-trod areas of '90s nostalgia: Saturday morning cartoons, Must-See TV, TGIF, Mike Myers movies, East Coast/West Coast rap wars, and so on. I thought researching this would be like walking through the '90s section of an imagined museum, everything preserved behind glass, curiosities whose time had come and gone. But what I discovered was how much of the world we're living in now was born in the '90s. Fast casual dining chains, the Tyler Durdenization of toxic masculinity, Putin's Russia, K-Pop boy bands who took much of their playbook from NSYNC and The Backstreet Boys, and much more; it's like the '90s never left ... for better or for worse.

I loved digging around for general knowledge and deeper trivia to challenge and inform you. Feel free to wow your friends and coworkers with the knowledge within! I hope you have as much fun answering these questions and solving these puzzles as I did creating them.

Cowabunga,
—Buzzy

Quiz 1: ¡Qué Linda!

1. What was the name of Monica Lewinsky's pal who secretly recorded their conversations?

2. Who was the host of "Coffee Talk" on *Saturday Night Live*? Played by Mike Myers, when she would get verklempt she'd give the audience a topic to discuss while collecting herself.

3. She won the 1990 Grammy for Best Pop Performance by a Duo or Group for a song she recorded with Aaron Neville, then did the same one year later. What's her name (and what were the songs)?

4. Linda Perry has written for many other artists (including Top 10 singles for Christina Aguilera and Pink), but her first big hit was 1993's "What's Up?" for her own band. What was their name?

5. Linda Claridge is better known by what last name? She was married to her now ex-husband in the '80s and through the '90s, during which he left the WWF to join the recently formed WCW.

6. Linda Emery's famous husband passed away in 1973. Sadly, her famous son also died young in 1993 on the set of the film that would become synonymous with his name. Name both her son and the film, which was released posthumously in 1994.

7. What newswoman became the lead anchor of Nick News when it was launched by Nickelodeon in 1992?

8. Which Beatle married Linda Eastman, who started an eponymous vegetarian frozen food company in 1991?

9. Linda Larkin made her first film appearance in 1990's straight-to-video sequel *Zapped Again!*, but she is most famous for being the speaking voice for what Disney princess who debuted in 1992?

10. Linda Hamilton reprised her role as what character in 1991's *Terminator 2: Judgment Day*?

11. Christy Turlington, Naomi Campbell, and what Linda formed "the Trinity" of '90s supermodels?

12. Lynda Carter may have played Wonder Woman back in the '70s, but we '90s kids remember her as someone who "wouldn't trust these baby blues to just anyone" in a series of ads for what company?

Answers on page 97.

Quiz 2: The Disney Afternoon

1. *TaleSpin* features characters from what 1967 animated film?

2. Who was "the terror that flaps in the night," per the opening monologue of every episode of the eponymous show?

3. In *Chip 'n Dale: Rescue Rangers*, the two Disney characters borrowed some personality and swag from what two famous human characters? Chip wore a bomber jacket and fedora in homage to one, and Dale sported a red and yellow Hawaiian shirt reminiscent of the other.

4. What was the name of Goofy's son on *Goof Troop*?
   a) Jack
   b) Fido
   c) Max
   d) Cliff

5. The original *DuckTales* aired its final episode in November of 1990, but after the success of *Goof Troop*, a new show was launched in 1996 featuring Donald and older versions of his nephews. What was it called?
   a) *Duck Bunch*
   b) *Quack Pack*
   c) *Don's Crew*
   d) *Absurd Mallards*

6. What three shows from the Disney Afternoon were inspired by hit feature films from the so-called Disney Renaissance of the late '80s and '90s?

7. Somewhere deep in your brain you may remember the cartoon about a bobcat who is a crime-solving cop in Hollywood ... but can you remember his name?

8. What was the only Disney Afternoon animated series inspired by a live-action film?

9. Which of the following was *not* a Gummi Bear: Zummi Gummi, Yummi Gummi, Tummi Gummi, Gruffi Gummi, Grammi Gummi, Sunni Gummi, or Cubbi Gummi?

10. Other than Goliath and Demona, the "Manhattan Clan" of the Gargoyles from the animated series *Gargoyles* were all named after New York geographical landmarks. How many can you name?

Answers on pages 97–98.

Bonus: *DuckTales* Details

Can you match the first and last names of these *DuckTales* characters?

1. Bentina	**a.** Beagle
2. Benzino	**b.** Beakley
3. Farley	**c.** Crackshell
4. Fenton	**d.** Cronduck
5. Fergus	**e.** De Spell
6. Flintheart	**f.** Foghorn
7. Gladstone	**g.** Gander
8. Gloria	**h.** Gassolini
9. Goldie	**i.** Gearloose
10. Gyro	**j.** Glomgold
11. John D.	**k.** McDuck
12. Launchpad	**l.** McQuack
13. Ludwig	**m.** O'Gilt
14. Ma	**n.** Rockefeather
15. Magica	**o.** Swansong
16. Oprah	**p.** Van Honk
17. Vacation	**q.** Vanderquack
18. Walter	**r.** Von Drake
19. Webby	**s.** Walters
20. Webra	**t.** Webfeet

Answers on page 98.

Quiz 3: Bo Knows

1. Bo Knows Baseball! Bo Jackson started out playing for the Kansas City Royals before moving to the Chicago White Sox, but his final MLB season in 1994 was with what team?

2. Bo Knows Football! Bo Jackson was selected by the Tampa Bay Buccaneers as the #1 draft pick in 1986, but he turned them down. He was then selected as the 183rd draft pick the following year by which team?

3. Which brand ran the iconic "Bo Knows" ad campaign?
a) Reebok
b) Nike
c) Adidas
d) Puma

4. During the first "Bo Knows" spot, Bo demonstrated his knowledge of many things, vouched for in most cases by a star of that sport. How many of the speakers of these lines from the commercial can you name?
a) "Bo knows baseball"
b) "Bo knows football"
c) "Bo knows basketball, too"
d) "Bo knows tennis?"
e) "Bo knows running!"
f) "No" (he was supposed to say "Bo knows hockey")

5. What two other things did Bo know, per the ad?

6. Complete this line from the end of the commercial, in which the guitarist who's been playing throughout the ad comments on Bo Jackson's guitar skills: "Bo, you don't know ___!"

Answers on page 99.

Quiz 4: 90210

1. What was the name of the high school the protagonists attended?
   a) Beverly Hills High
   b) North Beverly High
   c) West Beverly High
   d) Beverly Central High

2. What was the name of the '50s-style restaurant that's the hangout for the teens?

3. Steve convinced Nat, owner of the aforementioned restaurant, to open up a nightclub next door (which was partially financed by Dylan). Many real-life artists performed at the club as part of the show, including Christina Aguilera, Luther Vandross, and the Flaming Lips. What was the club called?

4. Twins Brenda and Brandon moved to Beverly Hills after previously living in what state?

5. While the majority of the cast are sophomores in Season 1, which member of the gang is a freshman?

6. Which character was played by the daughter of the show's executive producer?

7. Who decides for financial reasons (but also probably to keep the character in the show) to not attend Yale but instead attend California University with the rest of the cast?

8. Which two characters' parents met and got married, making them step-siblings (much to the chagrin of one of them)?

9. Valerie Malone joined the show in Season 5. This sometimes manipulative character with a checkered past was played by what actress, known primarily for being a cast member of another, albeit lighter-hearted, teen show?

10. Which character opened the clothing boutique "Now Wear This" where they displayed their designs?

11. Match each character below to their car:

1. Brandon	a. BMW convertible
2. Brenda	b. Corvette
3. Dylan	c. Mercury Cougar a.k.a. "Mondale"
4. Kelly	d. Porsche
5. Steve	e. No car (didn't pass their driver's test)

Answers on page 99.

Bonus: One and Done

Some of the most beloved '90s TV shows only lasted one season. Who could forget *My So-Called Life* (1994–95) and *Freaks and Geeks* (1999–2000), which launched so many careers? Or sketch comedies like 1992–93's *The Ben Stiller Show* (which had the distinction of winning a writing Emmy *after* being canceled) or 1996's *The Dana Carvey Show* (which memorably featured Steve Carell and Stephen Colbert playing two waiters nauseated by food)? Of the one-season wonders below, each debuted in a different year of the 1990s. Can you put them in order from 1990 to 1999?

- *The Adventures of Brisco County, Jr.*, starring Bruce Campbell (27 episodes)
- *All-American Girl*, starring Margaret Cho (19 episodes)
- *Cop Rock*, featuring a theme song by Randy Newman (11 episodes)
- *Cupid*, starring Paula Marshall and Jeremy Piven (15 episodes)
- *Drexell's Class*, starring Dabney Coleman (18 episodes)
- *EZ Streets*, starring Ken Olin and Joe Pantoliano (9 episodes, one unaired)
- *George & Leo*, starring Bob Newhart and Judd Hirsch (22 episodes)
- *Harsh Realm*, by *X-Files* creator Chris Carter (9 episodes)
- *The Heights*, created by Aaron Spelling, and whose "How Do You Talk to an Angel" by the titular band was the first single by a fictional band to hit #1 since the Archies' "Sugar Sugar" (13 episodes, one unaired)
- *Nowhere Man*, starring Bruce Greenwood (25 episodes)

Answers on page 100.

Quiz 5: SNICK

1. *Clarissa Explains It All* opened up the original SNICK lineup. What was the name of her mischievous, red-headed, Young Republican little brother?

2. Which SNICK program featured the theme music "Hey Sandy," performed by indie rock band Polaris?

3. What sci-fi show joined the line-up in October 1994 and starred Larisa Oleynik, who is also well known for playing the younger Stratford sister, Bianca, in 1999's *10 Things I Hate About You*?

4. What was the name of the horror anthology series that aired late (hey, 9:30 is late-night if you're a kid!) and featured members of the Midnight Society telling each other scary stories?

5. For its first four years, SNICK featured one animated program, the third of the network's "Nicktoons." It was a huge hit, though not without controversy due to its dark humor, adult themes, and sexual innuendo. What was this program that aired at 9 p.m. on Saturday nights?

6. What SNICK sketch comedy show, a kids' version of *Saturday Night Live*, originated the "Good Burger" sketch that was later spun off into a feature film?

7. Speaking of "Good Burger," the stars of that sketch had their own comedy series spun off as part of SNICK in October 1996. Name their first names and you name the show; who are they?

8. For its first few years SNICK had a comedy variety show that would end every episode with a cast member saying "Reprise the theme and roll the credits!" What was the name of this show (which refers to the building where railroad companies would turn trains around, and not a martial arts kick)?

9. SNICK had a long line of shows with strong female leads, starting with *Clarissa Explains It All.* What show, which premiered in 1996 starring Irene Ng as the eponymous kid investigator, co-starred "Mr. Miyagi" himself, Pat Morita, as the main character's grandfather?

10. SNICK was a replacement for what regular programming block that usually came on Nickelodeon in the evenings and played reruns of old sitcoms?

Answers on page 100.

Bonus: Alternative Bands

I've taken the '90s bands below even further from the mainstream by replacing each letter in their names with an alternative letter, cryptogram-style. Substitutions are consistent throughout the list. Can you decode them all?

MQDLTBOITCL

UOLTWCHQV

ECWKRLM

ACOIW FOE

HCL JQWTM JRKC

EDTYQLCP

ARVRCM

BDRTCT HP KQRUCM

MWCOSCI-XRLLCP

LCDSIOW ERWX YQSCW

MEOMYRLB ADEAXRLM

CWOMSRUO

FOLC'M OTTRUSRQL

SCCLOBC JOLUWDH

KCIDUO MOWS

Answers on page 101.

Quiz 6: '90s Potpourri #1

1. Sergei Krikalev, known as "the last Soviet citizen," had what job during the dissolution of the Soviet Union?

2. From 1992 to 1994, Harrison Ford depicted what Tom Clancy character (who was previously portrayed by Alec Baldwin, and has since been portrayed by Ben Affleck, Chris Pine, and John Krasinski)?

3. What Texas billionaire ran as a third-party candidate in the 1992 presidential race and ended up winning 18.9% of the popular vote?

4. What former world leader appeared in an iconic and unexpected commercial for Pizza Hut in 1998?

5. The steroid era of baseball was wild, huh? In 1998, what two players were in a race to defeat Roger Maris's home run record? (And which one won?)

6. What football team reached the Super Bowl in four consecutive years (1990–93), losing all four of them?

7. Despite its long and storied history going back to the 1920s, Mercedes-Benz's best-selling model of all time is what compact-executive car introduced in 1993?

8. What fictional British spy was frozen in 1967 and unfrozen in 1997 to defeat his archnemesis (who had returned from his own spaceborne frozen hibernation)?

9. In what city do Wayne Campbell and Garth Algar live? Their show *Wayne's World* was initially broadcast on that city's public access station.

10. While Arnold Schwarzenegger will always be remembered as "the Governator," what former wrestler and fellow cast member in *Predator* and *The Running Man* won the 1998 governor's race in Minnesota?

11. 1992 was the last year in which the Winter and Summer Olympics were held in the same year. What two cities hosted these games?

12. In 1992, then-president George H.W. Bush, while attending a banquet, threw up in the lap of the dinner host, who happened to be the prime minister of what country?

13. While the cocker spaniel spent the '80s and entered the '90s as the most popular dog breed in North America, in 1992 it was overtaken by what larger breed?

14. Ryan Schreiber started a music review website in 1996 named *Turntable*. He relaunched it later the same year with what new name, inspired by Tony Montana's tattoo from the film *Scarface*?

15. In 1992, what former Eastern Bloc state peacefully split into two countries, each retaining roughly half of the former country's name?

16. What was the name of the devastating hurricane that struck Florida and Louisiana in August of 1992?
a) Arnold
b) Alan
c) Andrew
d) Alex

17. What was the real name of the young woman dubbed by tabloids as "the Long Island Lolita"?

18. The first ever space telescope was launched in 1990 and named after what American astronomer?
a) Edwin Hubble
b) Carl Sagan
c) Maria Mitchell
d) Benjamin Banneker

19. What annual event was launched in 1995 by ESPN as something of an Olympics of extreme sports?

20. What pro surfer won his first competition at the 1990 Body Glove Surfbout at Trestles Beach in San Diego, California?

21. The official ball of the 1998 FIFA World Cup was produced by Adidas and named what, after a symbol of the host country?

22. What Jonathan Larson musical, which opened off-Broadway in 1996 and swiftly moved to Broadway, was based on Puccini's *La Bohème*?

23. Another hit '90s Broadway musical based on Puccini, *Miss Saigon* retells which opera (moving the setting to 1970s Vietnam)?

24. Disney Theatrical Productions was founded in 1994 to bring the film studio's films to the stage. Two hit films were adapted in the '90s into hit Broadway musicals—which were they?

25. While Margaret Thatcher was technically the first prime minister of the U.K. of the '90s, she was replaced by one man in 1990 (from the Conservative party) who served until replaced by another in 1997 (from the Labour party). Who were they?

Answers on pages 101–102.

Bonus: '90s Book-to-Movie Adaptations

1. 1995 book by Nicholas Evans inspired by horse trainer Buck Brannaman → 1998 film directed by and starring Robert Redford

2. 1991 novel by Bret Easton Ellis about an investment banker → 2000 film starring Christian Bale

3. 1996 novel by Jacquelyn Mitchard about a young boy's kidnapping → 1999 film starring Michelle Pfeiffer

4. 1998 YA novel by Louis Sachar about someone going to a correctional boot camp → 2003 film starring Sigourney Weaver, Jon Voight, Patricia Arquette, Tim Blake Nelson, and Shia LaBeouf

5. 1999 historical novel by Tracy Chevalier centering around the Delft painter Johannes Vermeer → 2003 film starring Scarlett Johansson

6. 1996 novel in the form of a personal journal by Helen Fielding → 2001 film starring Renee Zellweger

7. 1990 sci-fi novel by Michael Crichton about a unique cloning experiment → 1993 film directed by Stephen Spielberg

8. 1992 novel by Cormac McCarthy about two friends who go to Mexico on horseback to work as cowboys → 2000 film starring Matt Damon, Penélope Cruz, and directed by Billy Bob Thornton

9. 1996 novel by Terry McMillan about the eponymous character going to Jamaica → 1998 film starring Angela Bassett and Taye Diggs

10. 1992 romance novel by Robert James Waller about a WWII war bride living in Iowa → 1995 film starring Meryl Streep and Clint Eastwood (who also directed it)

11. 1996 roman à clef about Bill Clinton's 1992 campaign, published anonymously (but revealed later that year to have been written by columnist Joe Klein) → 1998 film starring John Travolta, Emma Thompson, and Billy Bob Thornton, directed by Mike Nichols

12. 1998 novel by Tom Perrotta about a girl running for student body president → 1999 film starring Reese Witherspoon and Matthew Broderick

13. 1996 novel by Chuck Palahniuk about a man struggling with insomnia ... kind of → 1999 David Fincher film starring Ed Norton, Brad Pitt, and Helena Bonham Carter

14. 1993 collection of short stories by Irvine Welsh about addicts living in Edinburgh →1996 Danny Boyle film starring Ewan MacGregor

15. 1992 novella by A.S. Byatt about a Victorian naturalist → 1995 film starring Mark Rylance, Patsy Kensit, and Kristin Scott Thomas

16. 1998 novel by Daniel Wallace about a son trying to understand who his raconteur father really was → 2003 Tim Burton film starring Ewan McGregor (and many others)

Answers on page 103.

Quiz 7: Drink Up!

1. Launched in 1992, what was the name of the clear cola drink from PepsiCo, which had basically the same formula as Pepsi-Cola, only without the caramel color? It was launched with an ad campaign featuring "Right Now" by Van Halen.

2. Part of the same "clear craze" that brought us the above-mentioned soda, what alcoholic malt beverage was introduced in 1993 as a clear alternative to beer? Its name means "winter" in many Slavic languages, and its tart, citrusy, sweet flavor paved the way for other malt beverages like Smirnoff Ice.

3. In 1997, Coca-Cola launched a product to compete with Pepsi's Mountain Dew, which leaned into hardcore and edgy branding. Discontinued in 2003, fan campaigns have resulted in a few limited revivals since 2014. What was the name of this iconic '90s soft drink?

4. Snapple made its debut in the '70s with a carbonated apple juice drink (hence the name), but it was their bottled teas and ads featuring the "Snapple Lady" that catapulted them to near ubiquity in the '90s (peach was my favorite, while my sister preferred raspberry). And during its '90s heyday, the labels on Snapple iced tea bottles featured images of what historic event?

5. Launched in 1992, this beverage company, which became known for its 23-ounce "Big Can," was given a name that did not reflect the fact that it was based in New York (just like its rival/inspiration Snapple), nor that the co-founder who named it had never traveled west of the Mississippi. Can you state its name?

6. How many iced tea brands were launched in the '90s?! This one from Lipton had an ad campaign that featured claymation versions of celebrities.

7. Released in 1997, this drink featured what can only be described as ... well, *chunks*, which were in actuality made out of something called gellan gum. Boba (a.k.a. bubble tea) has made this seem less strange in retrospect, but at the time, it was a very unusual experience. What was the name of this drink that asked you to chew while you drank?

8. Which three of the following beverages were considered but passed over in the fridge in favor of "Sunny D" in a famous Sunny Delight advertisement?
   a) O.J.
   b) Milk
   c) Apple juice
   d) Soda
   e) Water
   f) Purple stuff
   g) Iced tea
   h) Beer

9. The 1998 film *The Big Lebowski* quickly achieved cult status and popularized what drink made with Kahlua, vodka, and cream?

10. What bright green cocktail was created in 1996 at the West Hollywood restaurant Lola's by a bartender named Adam Karsten?

11. When *Sex and the City* debuted, it had every young (or not) single (or not) woman (or not) ordering this cocktail of vodka, Cointreau, lime juice, and cranberry juice. What is it?

12. In 1990, what beer brand introduced a Christmas ad featuring someone whistling "O Tannenbaum" while a palm tree becomes illuminated with Christmas lights? In 1998, it became the U.S.'s top-selling import beer.

13. What soft drink was introduced in 1999 by PepsiCo to compete with Coca-Cola's Sprite and 7up (which had merged with Dr Pepper the decade before)?

14. Named for a 19th-century national hero of its home country of Poland, this quadruple-distilled spirit was created in 1992 and introduced to the North American market in 1997. What is its name?

15. Long before today's glut of IPAs, the Coors Brewing Company wanted to tap into the growing craft beer market, which they did in 1995 with the introduction of a Belgian-style wheat beer. What's the name of this not-so-rare beer often served with an orange wheel?

16. While *Zoolander* made the fictional "orange mocha" variety of this drink infamous in 2001, it was actually launched by Starbucks in 1995, with its name being a portmanteau of two other popular coffee drinks.

17. Woodford Reserve has a name that feels like it reaches back generations, but this spirit brand was actually launched in 1993 as a rebranding of an old distillery of what type of liquor?

18. Soft-drink giants Coca-Cola, PepsiCo, and Dr Pepper each launched bottled water brands in the '90s, two of which have become staples of vending machines and airports. The third, not so much, though it should sound familiar. Can you remember their names (and their associated brands)?

 Answers on pages 103–104.

Bonus: Mixed Drinks

In each puzzle below, two 1990s beverages have been blended together by having their letters intermingled without rearranging them. For example, the letter sequence PECOPSKIE contains Pepsi and Coke: **PE**CO**PS**K**I**E. Can you figure out all of the ingredients in these mixed drinks?

1. SCURITGERA
2. SMIOSTIBEC
3. ZOIKSMOADA
4. TJYONASTNAT
5. OJROLBTICOTLZA
6. FSRUQUITEOPIEZAIT
7. SMALIRLNOSPFOFRICTE
8. KLOIFOLAESIADVERBSUSORDSATS
9. FHIRECSCECAPETACHOCOCITORLEURS
10. MOCULENARTLAINYDECAWSNAPODIRANT

Answers on pages 104–105.

Quiz 8: Trivia About Nothing ... Except *Seinfeld*

1. What candy did Kramer accidentally drop into a patient while viewing a surgery from the operating theater?

2. What was the name George often used as his alter ego?

3. George and Jerry's fictional show about nothing is called what?

4. What is Kramer's first name?

5. After passing through a few different jobs, including assistant to the head of Pendant Publishing, Elaine lands a job as a writer for (and, briefly, acting president of) a fictionalized version of what real-life publication?

6. On what arcade game, located at the pizza shop he frequented in high school, did George hold the all-time high score?

7. What's the name of Kramer's lawyer, who was loosely based on Johnnie Cochran?

8. What is the name of the holiday Frank Costanza invented as an alternative to Christmas and Hanukkah, which features such traditions as an aluminum pole, feats of strength, and the airing of grievances?

9. While he always seemed unemployed, it was revealed that Kramer had in fact been on strike for years from what famous New York establishment?

10. When Elaine's favorite type of contraception was discontinued, she was forced to decide which of the men she dated were worthy of depleting her large but limited cache of it. What was it?

11. After accidentally agreeing to wear a shirt designed by Kramer's girlfriend on television, Jerry exclaims that he doesn't want to be a what (which the shirt makes him resemble)?

12. What job is held by Jerry and Kramer's neighbor Newman?

13. George's fiancée Susan dies as a result of poisoning from what?

14. George purchased a used Chrysler LeBaron that he believed was owned by which actor?

15. What's the name of the coffee shop where the gang hangs out?

16. George Steinbrenner and Frank Costanza's lawyer (who wore a cape) were both portrayed by whom?

17. In two different episodes, Kramer made two figures out of pasta and presented them to their namesakes, one for Jerry and one for a celebrity playing herself. What were they (and what was Kramer's reason for his choice of pasta for Jerry)?

18. It was never revealed who won "The Contest" by remaining master of their domain the longest, but who were the first two people to lose?

Answers on pages 105–106.

Bonus: I Wish That I Had Jerry's Girl

Jerry went through a lot of girlfriends on *Seinfeld*, which I suppose is inevitable when your deal-breakers include things like "eating peas one at a time." Exactly half of the 32 actresses below guest-starred as one of those girlfriends; can you remember which ones?

- ☐ Gillian Anderson
- ☐ Jennifer Aniston
- ☐ Christina Applegate
- ☐ Angela Bassett
- ☐ Lara Flynn Boyle
- ☐ Jennifer Coolidge
- ☐ Courteney Cox
- ☐ Kristin Davis
- ☐ Laura Dern
- ☐ Janeane Garofalo
- ☐ Jami Gertz
- ☐ Lauren Graham
- ☐ Anna Gunn
- ☐ Teri Hatcher
- ☐ Helen Hunt
- ☐ Holly Hunter
- ☐ Victoria Jackson
- ☐ Catherine Keener
- ☐ Jane Leeves
- ☐ Jennifer Jason Leigh
- ☐ Lori Loughlin
- ☐ Virginia Madsen
- ☐ Marlee Matlin
- ☐ Debra Messing
- ☐ Alyssa Milano
- ☐ Julianne Moore
- ☐ Sarah Jessica Parker
- ☐ Amanda Peet
- ☐ Jeri Ryan
- ☐ Christine Taylor
- ☐ Ali Wentworth
- ☐ Catherine Zeta-Jones

Answers on page 106.

Quiz 9: Get a Clue

1. What song, performed by the Muffs, plays over the opening sequence of the film *Clueless*?

2. Tai (Brittany Murphy's character) insults Cher (Alicia Silverstone) by calling her a what who can't what?

3. The plot of *Clueless* is based on what Jane Austen novel?

4. What actor (and 2021's Sexiest Man Alive, per *People* magazine) plays Cher's ex-stepbrother Josh in his first big-screen role?

5. Donald Faison played Dionne's boyfriend, but is arguably more recognizable for his role in what 2000s sitcom?

6. What kind of car does Cher have (in spite of not having her license)?

7. What Coolio song is playing at the party in the Valley where Tai and the the dreamy Elton Tiscia romantically connect? Tai later tearfully sings part of the song in an emotional moment.

8. Ever the matchmaker, Cher is also trying to set up two teachers, Ms. Geist and Mr. Hall. Mr. Hall was played by character actor Wallace Shawn, who is perhaps best remembered for playing Vizzini in what cult favorite film?

9. Writer/director Amy Heckerling not only defined the '90s with *Clueless*, but the '80s as well with what high school comedy starring Sean Penn as perennial slacker Spicoli?

10. What is the name of the new student who gives Cher hope for high school boys, only for her to learn that he is gay?

11. When recently rhinoplastied student Amber informs the P.E. teacher that her plastic surgeon doesn't want her doing any activities where "Balls are flying at [her] face," Dionne responds with what quip?

12. What is Cher's most famous catchphrase, which was the title of a book compiling an "oral history" of the film, published on the 20th anniversary of its release?

13. Alicia Silverstone reprised her role as Cher Horowitz in a 2023 Super Bowl ad for what cash-back shopping app?

14. Which four of these actors reprised their film roles in the 1996–99 *Clueless* sitcom?

a) Alicia Silverstone
b) Stacey Dash
c) Elisa Donovan
d) Brittany Murphy
e) Dan Hedaya
f) Donald Faison
g) Wallace Shawn

Answers on page 106.

Bonus: To Explore Strange New Prosthetics

The Star Trek universe boomed in the 1990s; between *The Next Generation*, *Deep Space Nine*, and *Voyager*, there was always at least one series on the air every year. Naturally, that expansion produced many new characters (and new alien species). Can you match these characters with their species—or, in some cases, their technology?

1. Chakotay
2. Data
3. Elim Garak
4. Guinan
5. Ikat'ika
6. Jadzia Dax
7. Kes
8. Kira Nerys
9. Lwaxana Troi
10. Morn
11. Mot
12. Naomi Wildman
13. Neelix
14. Odo
15. Quark
16. Seven of Nine
17. The Caretaker (a.k.a. Banjo Man)
18. The Doctor (a.k.a the EMH)
19. Tuvix
20. Tuvok
21. Weyoun
22. Worf

- **a.** Bajoran
- **b.** Betazoid
- **c.** Bolian
- **d.** Borg, formerly human
- **e.** Cardassian
- **f.** Changeling
- **g.** El-Aurian
- **h.** Ferengi
- **i.** Half human, half Ktarian
- **j.** Half Vulcan, half Talaxian (due to a transporter accident)
- **k.** Hologram
- **l.** Human
- **m.** Jem'Hadar
- **n.** Klingon
- **o.** Lurian
- **p.** Nacene
- **q.** Ocampa
- **r.** Soong-type android
- **s.** Talaxian
- **t.** Trill
- **u.** Vorta
- **v.** Vulcan

Answers on page 107.

Quiz 10: The Clinton Years

1. Prior to becoming President, Bill Clinton had served as governor for which state?
   a) Texas
   b) Missouri
   c) Arkansas
   d) Oklahoma

2. The Clinton administration saw the appointment of the first female attorney general; which woman held this distinction?
   a) Janet Reno
   b) Condoleezza Rice
   c) Christine Todd Whitman
   d) Madeleine Albright

3. Vice President Al Gore was incorrectly quoted as claiming to have invented what technology?

4. First Lady (and future senator and presidential candidate) Hillary Clinton made what issue her focus in the beginning of the Clinton administration?

5. What controversial policy regarding gay and lesbian military service members was put into place during the Clinton years?

6. Robert Reich, who had served in previous administrations and would go on to serve on Obama's economic transition advisory board, held which cabinet position under Clinton?
   a) Secretary of Health and Human Services
   b) Secretary of the Treasury
   c) Secretary of Commerce
   d) Secretary of Labor

7. While I mainly remember James Carville as one of cable news's more memorable talking heads, he had been a political strategist who worked on Bill Clinton's successful 1992 campaign. He told folks working on the campaign to just focus on three messages: "Change vs. more of the same," "Don't forget healthcare," and what third one, which is by far the most famous?

8. Speaking of the '92 election, Clinton uttered an equally memorable phrase, claiming he didn't what?

9. The 1993 Battle of Mogadishu was dramatized in what 2001 Ridley Scott film?

10. What two justices did Clinton successfully nominate to the Supreme Court?

11. Clinton was said to have been in power during an economy that was neither too hot with inflation nor too cold with deflation. This type of economy is named after what fairy tale character?

12. With technology rapidly changing media, Clinton signed the DMCA into law in 1998. What does DMCA stand for?

13. In 1995, NATO initiated Operation Deliberate Force, which was an attempt to end the siege of what capital city of Bosnia and Herzegovina?

14. What then-president of Yugoslavia became, in 1999, the first sitting head of state to be charged with war crimes?

15. President Clinton famously played what instrument on *The Arsenio Hall Show*?
a) Guitar
b) Saxophone
c) Piano
d) Trumpet

16. In 1996, Bill Clinton gave a press conference discussing the discovery of what NASA believed could be bacterial fossils in a meteorite from Mars. The next year, an edited excerpt of that press conference was used without authorization in what science fiction movie?

17. The Clinton campaign chose what hit song of 1977 to be their theme song?

18. What form of exercise did President Clinton do approximately three times a week, much to the chagrin of the secret service?
a) Bicycling
b) Boxing
c) Swimming
d) Jogging

Answers on pages 107–108.

Bonus: Count on Clinton

In the chart below, indicate which states Bill Clinton won in the 1992 presidential election. To give you a little help, each state's number of electoral votes at the time is indicated. (Clinton won with a total of 370.)

- Alabama 9 ☐
- Alaska 3 ☐
- Arizona 8 ☐
- Arkansas 6 ☐
- California 54 ☐
- Colorado 8 ☐
- Connecticut 8 ☐
- Delaware 3 ☐
- D.C. 3 ☐
- Florida 25 ☐
- Georgia 13 ☐
- Hawaii 4 ☐
- Idaho 4 ☐
- Illinois 22 ☐
- Indiana 12 ☐
- Iowa 7 ☐
- Kansas 6 ☐
- Kentucky 8 ☐
- Louisiana 9 ☐
- Maine 4 ☐
- Maryland 10 ☐
- Massachusetts 12 ☐
- Michigan 18 ☐
- Minnesota 10 ☐
- Mississippi 7 ☐
- Missouri 11 ☐
- Montana 3 ☐
- Nebraska 5 ☐
- Nevada 4 ☐
- New Hampshire 4 ☐
- New Jersey 15 ☐
- New Mexico 5 ☐
- New York 33 ☐
- North Carolina 14 ☐
- North Dakota 3 ☐
- Ohio 21 ☐
- Oklahoma 8 ☐
- Oregon 7 ☐
- Pennsylvania 23 ☐
- Rhode Island 4 ☐
- South Carolina 8 ☐
- South Dakota 3 ☐
- Tennessee 11 ☐
- Texas 32 ☐
- Utah 5 ☐
- Vermont 3 ☐
- Virginia 13 ☐
- Washington 11 ☐
- West Virginia 5 ☐
- Wisconsin 11 ☐
- Wyoming 3 ☐

Answers on page 108.

Quiz 11: Latin Lessons

1. Which of these was the lead single off of Ricky Martin's 1999 self-titled smash hit album?
   a) "Private Emotion"
   b) "Shake Your Bon Bon"
   c) "She's All I Ever Had"
   d) "Livin' la Vida Loca"

2. Which singer broke out in 1999 with her album *On the Six*? She was already successful as an actor before becoming one of the biggest stars of Latin Pop.

3. In addition to making a guest appearance on one of the songs for the abovementioned album, what male singer, already a huge star singing salsa music in Spanish, rode the crossover wave with "Need to Know"?

4. Enrique Iglesias's big crossover hit was featured in the film *Wild Wild West*. What was this song that introduced us to Julio's son and invited us to dance?

5. In addition to launching a number of Latin pop stars to mainstream audiences, the Latin Pop explosion of the late '90s also brought a number of older artists back into the limelight. What guitarist's album *Supernatural* sold over 15 million copies after its release in June 1999, 30 years after he and his band released their first album?

6. Speaking of *Supernatural,* which song from that album featured vocals from Rob Thomas of Matchbox 20 and went on to win Grammy awards for Record of the Year, Song of the Year, and Best Pop Collaboration with Vocals?

7. Though it preceded the Latin Pop wave of the late '90s, 1993's "Bidi Bidi Bom Bom" was nonetheless a huge hit for which singer of Tejano music?

8. Between his tenure in the boy band Menudo and his breakout as a solo artist in 1995, Ricky Martin joined the cast of what long-running soap opera in 1994?

9. What pop singer often recorded Spanish-language versions of her English-language releases, such as 1998's "Genio Atrapado"?

10. What Latin pop star of the 2020s was born in Puerto Rico in 1994? He made a guest appearance at the Super Bowl LIV halftime show in 2020 with Latin pop icons Shakira and Jennifer Lopez.

Answers on page 109.

Quiz 12: Hey Arnold!

Arnold Schwarzenegger was a box office powerhouse in the '90s, starring in blockbuster after blockbuster. Here are brief plot summaries of all the movies of the decade that he starred in; can you name them?

1. John Kruger, an elite U.S. Marshall working in the witness protection program, discovers a mole in his operation.

2. Douglas Quaid tries to piece together what is memory and what is fantasy as he uncovers a conspiracy on Mars.

3. Harry Tasker struggles to balance his family life with his job as a secret agent for the U.S. government.

4. A New York City cop must somehow protect an innocent woman from Satan, who wants her to be the mother of his child (that is, the Antichrist).

5. Dr. Alex Hesse undergoes the first male pregnancy. Hilarity ensues.

6. Detective John Kimble goes undercover to find the wife and child of a suspected drug dealer. Hilarity ensues.

7. Arnold plays Jack Slater (as well as himself) in this film parodying many of the characters he himself has portrayed, in which a magical ticket allows a young man to enter the world of the films he loves.

8. Two fathers go to desperate lengths to buy the highly sought-after Turbo-Man toy on Christmas Eve. Hilarity ensues.

9. A billionaire tries to undermine the efforts of two scientists, one looking to reverse global warming and the other trying to reforest the earth (ha).

10. A reprogrammed evil robot (so now a good robot) must protect the future leader of the human resistance from a more advanced evil robot.

While we're on the topic, below are the actors who played Arnold's foes in the above ten movies; can you match them all up?

a. Gabriel Byrne
b. James Caan
c. George Clooney
d. Ronny Cox
e. Charles Dance
f. Frank Langella
g. Art Malik
h. Robert Patrick
i. Sinbad
j. Richard Tyson

Answers on pages 109–110.

Bonus: Christina Vs. Britney

Don't worry, I won't make you pick your favorite. But of the following biographical facts, can you tell which ones describe Christina Aguilera, which describe Britney Spears, and which describe both?

1. Was a Mouseketeer on *The All-New Mickey Mouse Club*
2. Dated Justin Timberlake
3. Performed "Like a Virgin" with Madonna at the 2003 VMAs
4. Had one #1 hit in 1999
5. Appeared on the "Mulan" soundtrack
6. Has a Broadway musical based on her songs
7. Competed as a junior vocalist on *Star Search* (and did not win)
8. Was a judge on *The X Factor*
9. Was a coach on *The Voice*
10. Did "Carpool Karaoke" with James Corden
11. Won Best New Artist at the 2000 Grammy Awards
12. Lived in Japan for multiple years
13. Appeared as herself on *Glee*
14. Appeared as herself on *Entourage*
15. Was born in Mississippi
16. Dated back-up dancer Jorge Santos
17. Married back-up dancer Kevin Federline
18. Was signed to the label RCA
19. Had her vocals featured alongside the music from the Strokes' "Hard to Explain" in an early mash-up
20. Has been both a host and a musical guest on *Saturday Night Live*

Answers on pages 110–111.

Quiz 13: Let's Eat

1. What chain, founded in 1990 and known for having large communal tables, is French for "The Daily Bread"?

2. What juice chain, originally named Juice Club when it was launched in 1990 in San Luis Obispo, California, became much better known after changing its name to one said to be derived from a West African word for celebration?

3. Baja Fresh may have a name that evokes the Mexican cuisine served there, but it was actually founded in 1990 in which California city?
   a) Pismo Beach
   b) Newbury Park
   c) Encinitas
   d) Gualala

4. What restaurant chain was co-founded in 1991 by John Y. Brown Jr. (former CEO of KFC and governor of Kentucky from 1979 to 1983) and, more memorably, a country singer who was the restaurant's namesake?

5. While it never became a chain, this San Francisco restaurant that opened in 1991 became famous for its menu that featured garlic in every dish, including garlic ice cream. (It also became famous among cab drivers, who would reputedly refuse to pick up passengers there.) What is the name of this restaurant, derived from a nickname for garlic?

6. In 1991, Robert Earl launched Planet Hollywood in New York City. The restaurant was full of film memorabilia and was backed by three of Hollywood's biggest stars at the time. While many other actors would get involved later, what three leading men were part of the launch?

7. The popular Japanese-style restaurant Wagamama now has locations in over 20 countries, but the majority of its locations are in what country, where it was founded in 1992?

8. While not a chain or household name, the french restaurant Aubergine (which opened in the Chelsea district of London in 1993 and was eventually awarded two Michelin stars) launched the career of its head chef ... who *is* very much a household name. Who ran the kitchen there until 1998, when he and the staff staged a walkout?

9. What Italian chain's name translates loosely as "Joey's little place"?

10. When Steve Ells opened his first fast casual Mexican restaurant in Denver in 1993, he figured he needed to sell at least 107 burritos per day to be profitable; he was soon selling over 1,000. What is the name of the chain he started, which now has over 3,000 locations?

11. Liliana Lovell decided to quit her Wall Street internship for a more lucrative bartending job, and in 1993 opened her own bar, which became famous for bartop dancing. In addition to locations across the U.S. and beyond, the bar spawned a film produced by Jerry Bruckheimer, based on a *GQ* article written by author Elizabeth Gilbert, who had worked at the original location as a bartender. What is the name of the bar?

12. P.F. Chang's took its name from founders Paul Fleming (P.F.) and Philip Chiang (changed to Chang). In which Arizona city did this Asian fusion chain get its start?
   a) Phoenix
   b) Flagstaff
   c) Scottsdale
   d) Tucson

13. The '90s loved a themed restaurant; Planet Hollywood certainly wasn't alone. What jungle-themed spot made its debut in Minnesota in 1994?

14. What mall staple was launched in a California mall in 1994, eventually bringing its pretzels, hot dogs, and lemonade beyond the malls with over 200 locations, including outposts in both Disneyland and Walt Disney World?

15. With a punny interior design connection to the golden age of aviation, what chicken wing restaurant was launched in 1994 in Garland, Texas?

16. There are in fact no genius brothers behind this chain of bagel and coffee shops; it was actually created by Boston Chicken (later Boston Market) as a way to break into the breakfast food market. What was this restaurant, formed by combining and rebranding multiple, relatively smaller chains?

17. The first place that *I* ever had the now-extremely-popular soup dumpling (a.k.a. *xiaolongbao* or *tangbao*) was this famous chain that started out in Flushing, Queens. My first soupy bite was in the Pell Street location in New York's Chinatown, but if New York is too inconvenient, you can try one of its locations in Japan. What's this restaurant that I'm hardly unwilling to visit?

18. Another fast casual Mexican restaurant from Colorado, this spot, founded in 1995 as Zuma, underwent multiple name changes thanks to lawsuits from similarly named businesses. First it became Z-Teca in 1997, then, in 1999, changed to what invented name that would score 17 points in Scrabble if it were playable?

19. While Planet Hollywood tried to create an aura of showbiz proximity, this seafood chain immersed patrons directly in the world of one particular movie, taking its name from a company founded by two characters from 1994's Best Picture Oscar winner. What's the name of this restaurant where, incidentally, Chris Pratt was waiting tables when he was discovered at age 19 by Rae Dawn Chong?

20. What West Village bakery, founded in 1996, is credited with starting the cupcake craze, and was featured in *Sex and the City*, *The Devil Wears Prada*, and the viral *Saturday Night Live* digital short "Lazy Sunday"?

21. What smoothie franchise, founded in Los Angeles back in 1996 (and currently found in over 90 cities), features a hummingbird with a red head and a green body in its logo?

22. What sports bar chain founded in Long Beach in 1996 is reportedly named after a large Colonial-era beer glass capable of holding approximately 2.5 pints (and not, as you might assume, a physical location)?

23. In 1997, a French brasserie opened in the rapidly transforming TriBeCa district of Manhattan. What is the name of this restaurant that is part of the restaurant empire owned by Keith McNally, and that shares its name with one of the magi who bring gifts to baby Jesus, as well as with another large container of alcohol (in this case, a wine bottle that holds 12 liters)?

24. What coffee roaster, founded in 1999, is practically synonymous with Portland, Oregon? In addition to its own cafes, the company supplies beans to many high-end coffee shops and hotels such as New York's Ace Hotel, and was one of the first to put cold brew coffee into nitro cans.

Answers on page 111.

Bonus: Disemvoweled '90s Hip-Hop Songs

These hip-hop songs have been camouflaged in two ways: their vowels have been removed, and they have been respaced. So, for instance (to choose an older hip-hop classic), "Rapper's Delight" might be presented as RP PRSDL GHT. How many can you identify (and how many of the artists can you name)? Note that for the purposes of this puzzle, Y is never considered a vowel.

1. TW SGDDY
2. CLF RNL V
3. THHM PTYD NC
4. RGL T
5. NT HNB TGT HNG
6. THC RSSR DS
7. M KMS YHH
8. MMS DKN CKYT
9. MYN MS
10. JMPR ND
11. BC KTH TZZP
12. CNK CKT?
13. PSS NMBY
14. JCY
15. GNN DJC
16. NTR GLC TC

 Answers on page 112.

Quiz 14: Animaniac Mania

1. What are the names of the three Warner siblings who are the stars of *Animaniacs*?
   a) Groucho, Harpo, Chico
   b) Huey, Dewey, Louie
   c) Mama, Papa, Baby
   d) Yakko, Wakko, Dot

2. Where do the protagonists live on the Warner Bros. lot?

3. What is the catchphrase the characters use when seeing an attractive person?

4. What type of animal were the recurring "Goodfeathers," based on characters from films such as *GoodFellas* and *The Godfather*?
   a) Chickens
   b) Pigeons
   c) Ducks
   d) Crows

5. *Pinky and the Brain* was originally a recurring segment of *Animaniacs* before it was spun off into its own show. What did Pinky and the Brain (well, mostly the Brain) do every night?

6. Brain's voice was inspired by what old Hollywood actor/director?

7. What's the name of the grumpy old anthropomorphic squirrel who lives in a tree with her chipper nephew Skippy?

8. The "Buttons and Mindy" sequences feature a young girl getting into trouble and being rescued by her pet dog Buttons—who inevitably gets blamed for all of the chaos she creates. What breed of dog is Buttons?
   a) German shepherd
   b) Golden retriever
   c) Beagle
   d) St. Bernard

9. What is the name of the German-accented studio psychiatrist whose task it is to make the Warner siblings less zany?

10. What is the name of the hamster (voiced by Roddy McDowall) who had once been Brain's friend, but was now his greatest rival?

11. Mr. Skullhead was a character featured in which recurring segment?
   a) Good Idea, Bad Idea
   b) Wheel of Morality
   c) Cute Things That Can Kill You
   d) The Flame

12. Trivia lovers are particularly fond of two songs from the series. One of them, "Yakko's World," lists all—well, most—of the world's nations as of 1993 to the tune of "Jarabe Tapatío" (popularly known as "The Mexican Hat Dance"), although it includes numerous inaccuracies. More reliable as a mnemonic was another song, which listed what to the tune of "Turkey in the Straw"?

Answers on pages 112–113.

Quiz 15: ’90s Potpourri #2

1. What Israeli prime minister first held the post in the 1970s but then served again from 1992 until he was assassinated in 1995 by an ultranationalist who opposed his peace initiatives such as the signing of the Oslo Accords?
   a) David Ben-Gurion
   b) Menachem Begin
   c) Shimon Peres
   d) Yitzhak Rabin

2. What was the name of the controversial trilateral trade agreement enacted in 1994 in an effort to create a free-trade zone between Canada, Mexico, and the United States of America?

3. What Georgia Republican, who co-authored the “Contract With America” and was named *Time* magazine’s Person of the Year in 1995, was speaker of the House from that year until he stepped down in 1998 after the GOP’s unexpectedly poor election performance, resigning his House seat shortly thereafter in January 1999 (20 years to the day after he originally took office)?

4. What American politician of the ’90s was known for his gaffes, including, famously, encouraging a sixth-grade student to misspell “potato” by adding an “E” at the end?

5. The New Age UFO cult known as Heaven's Gate made headlines in 1997 when all members (including their leader Marshall Applewhite, a.k.a. "Do") participated in a mass suicide in hopes that their souls would "ascend" to the UFO they believed was hiding in what celestial object?

6. From February 28 to April 19, 1993, federal and state law enforcement officers laid siege to the headquarters of the Branch Davidians, led by David Koresh, just outside of what Texas town that would become synonymous with the event?

7. In 1996, British author, activist, and adventurer Jason Lewis became the first person to cross North America using what human-powered (and very 1990s) mode of transportation?

8. In 1992, The Cure hit #18 on *Billboard*'s Hot 100 with a song that was not their highest-charting single (that was 1989's "Lovesong," which reached #2), but did become their highest-selling overall, earning a 2× Platinum certification. What was this song, whose title represented a contrast with other days of the week that had drawbacks such as being blue (Monday) or gray (Tuesday and Wednesday both)?

9. Elizabeth Taylor started off the decade with the launch of what perfume? It was promoted with a cinematic ad featuring Ms. Taylor herself donning the item for which the fragrance was named and quickly became immensely successful, ushering in a new era of celebrity fragrances.

10. Since its introduction, what celebrity-endorsed product has sold over 100 million units worldwide, and spawned copycat products from boxer Evander Holyfield and track star Carl Lewis?

11. Introduced by furniture company Herman Miller in 1994, what futuristic and ergonomic chair has become nearly ubiquitous in offices and is part of the permanent collection of the Museum of Modern Art?

12. What business, now a leader in the streaming world, launched as a DVD-by-mail rental service in 1997?

13. A severe weather system in 1991 caused a number of delays and outages on the British Rail system. An interview with British Rail's director of operations on BBC Radio 4 suggested the cause was "the wrong kind of" what?

14. The April 1992 verdict in the case of the police beating of Rodney King, which failed to convict any of the four indicted officers, caused Los Angeles to erupt in historic riots that Rodney King himself attempted to calm at an impromptu press conference by asking what five-word question?

15. What product debuted a 1992 ad campaign that featured a rousing rendition of Aaron Copland's "Hoe-Down" and concluded with narrator Robert Mitchum delivering the slogan "____: it's what's for dinner"?

Answers on page 113.

Bonus: Celebrity Couples

Given the initials and a brief description, can you name each of the following '90s celebrity couples?

1. Met on the set of *Se7en*, got engaged two years later, then called off the engagement six months after that.

2. This model and actor were introduced in 1994 and were together for four years.

3. Met on the set of *Good Will Hunting*; she was later surprised when he announced on *Oprah* that he was single, which was news to her.

4. After meeting on the set of *Days of Thunder*, this couple was married in 1990 and appeared in two more films together before splitting up in 2001.

5. Though they wed in 1987 (in Las Vegas, on a whim), these two actors were one of the biggest power couples of the '90s.

6. This actor (then 42) married this supermodel (then 25) in 1991, also in an impromptu Las Vegas ceremony; they divorced in 1995.

7. This model/actress and this rock star redefined tabloid news when their sex tape leaked.

8. This film star and country singer tied the knot just three weeks after meeting in 1993, splitting amicably two years later.

9. This singer (represented here by the nickname by which she was then better known) met this athlete after one of his soccer matches in 1997, and they've been together ever since.

Answers on page 114.

Quiz 16: Screen Test

1. In the movie *Speed* Sandra Bullock and Keanu Reeves cannot let the bus get below what speed?

2. *Speed* was followed up with what some consider the worst sequel ever, *Speed 2: Cruise Control,* in which Sandra Bullock found herself on what kind of vehicle?

3. In the 1997 film *Face/Off*, what two actors "swap faces" thanks to an implausible surgical procedure? One of their characters is a homicidal sociopath and the other is an FBI agent hunting him down.

4. What 1993 film opens with Sylvester Stallone grabbing onto the gloved hand of a woman he is attempting to rescue after her climbing harness breaks, only for her to slip and fall to her death?

5. Ingmar Berman's 1957 film *The Seventh Seal* features a knight playing chess with Death for his life. What 1991 sequel parodied this with the protagonists challenging Death to games of Battleship, Clue, Electric Football, and Twister (and winning all of them)?

6. What was the only *Star Wars* film released in the 1990s?

7. What 1993 comedy starred Pauly Shore as "Crawl," a spaced-out Californian who experiences culture clash when he spends Thanksgiving with his friend Becca's family in South Dakota?

8. What's the name of the women's baseball team that's the focus of 1992's *A League of Their Own*?
   a) The Rockford Comets
   b) The Rockford Blue Sox
   c) The Rockford Peaches
   d) The Rockford Belles

9. What 1998 film featured Matt Damon and Ed Norton playing underground high stakes poker?

10. Despite the title, Nicole Kidman is featured with her eyes open on the poster for this 1999 film, which was director Stanley Kubrick's last. What was it?

11. 1999's *Being John Malkovich* starred John Cusack as a frustrated artist working in what field?

12. Pixar Animation's first feature-length film was released in 1995. One of the challenges of early computer animation was that it was hard to make things that had realistic textures, and everything had a super-smooth, plastic look. What was the name of this first film which used this weakness of the medium as a strength?

13. What 1996 cult superhero film based on a comic book starred Pamela Anderson as the titular nightclub-owner-slash-mercenary-slash-bounty-hunter?

14. Richard Curtis wrote many hit films in which Hugh Grant starred, including *Bridget Jones's Diary*, *Notting Hill*, and *Love, Actually*—but their first collaboration was what 1994 film centered around five major life events?

15. The three James Bond films released in the '90s all starred what actor?

a) Pierce Brosnan
b) Timothy Dalton
c) George Lazenby
d) Daniel Craig

16. Marisa Tomei had her breakout performance as Mona Lisa Vito in what 1992 film in which she co-starred with Joe Pesci and Ralph Macchio?

17. In 1998's Best Picture Oscar winner *Shakespeare in Love*, Viola de Lesseps disguises herself as a man so she can audition for William Shakespeare's next play; he falls for her when he discovers her true identity. What play were they rehearsing? (And what two actors portrayed the star-crossed pair of lovers?)

18. The Spice Girls craze culminated in the movie *Spice World*, which featured all of the following celebrities but one. Who is the odd one out?

a) Meat Loaf
b) Elvis Costello
c) Alan Cumming
d) Roger Moore
e) Sting
f) Elton John
g) Jennifer Saunders

19. In 1991's *The Silence of the Lambs*, Hannibal Lecter claims to have eaten someone's liver "with some fava beans and a nice Chianti." What was that person's profession?

 Answers on page 114.

Bonus: Oh, Boy Bands

Can you match up all the boy band members with their bands?

98 Degrees **Backstreet Boys** **Boyz II Men** **NSYNC**

Lance Bass

Nick Carter

JC Chasez

Howie Dorough

Joey Fatone

Justin Jeffre

Chris Kirkpatrick

Drew Lachey

Nick Lachey

Brian Littrell

AJ McLean

Wanyá Morris

Kevin Richardson

Shawn Stockman

Justin Timberlake

Jeff Timmons

Michael McCary

Nathan Morris

Answers on page 115.

Quiz 17: (Small) Screen Test

1. What iconic show, which launched a number of spinoff series (eventually encompassing over 1,300 episodes among all its versions), debuted in 1990 on NBC? It was created by Dick Wolf, with unmistakable theme music—and an even more unmistakable "dun-dun" sound—by Mike Post.

2. Also debuting on NBC in 1990 was this story all about how the main character's life got flipped, turned upside down. The opening theme was performed by the show's star, telling the story of his relocation both across the country and across the socio-economic spectrum. What was the show, and who was the star whose life it was loosely based on?

3. What show featured the theme song "Tossed Salad and Scrambled Eggs," and who performed it?

4. What '90s drama featured main character Mitch Buchannon and a rotating cast of many others keeping folks safe while keeping things hot? (You may be surprised to learn that C.J. wasn't part of the first season—she didn't join the show until season 3. But do you remember what else was different about the first season?)

5. What all-male a cappella group performed the theme song for *Where in the World is Carmen Sandiego?*

6. In 1991, the former mayor of Cincinnati started a daytime talk show. While it initially had a fairly highbrow political bent, after a few years it went for more of a sensational tabloid approach, with fights frequently erupting and the audience chanting the host's name as chaos ensued. In spite of this, he ended every show by saying "Take care of yourselves and each other." Who on earth was the host of this show?

7. What former actress, who appeared in a number of John Waters films, launched her own daytime talk show in 1993?

8. What hit animated series was based on two animated shorts the creators made for the holidays, the second of which became one of the first viral videos on the Internet? The show begins with a disclaimer which ends with "The following program contains coarse language and due to its content it should not be viewed by anyone."

9. *Dallas* had "Who Shot J.R.?," but *The Simpsons* had their own whodunit: 1995's "Who Shot Mr. Burns?" ended the sixth season of the hit show on a cliffhanger; when part two aired four months later to kick off season 7, who did it turn out was the culprit?
   a) Smithers
   b) Homer
   c) Bart
   d) Maggie

10. What colors were the five original Mighty Morphin Power Rangers?

11. Rob Morrow starred in what CBS show about a recent med school grad sent to practice in Alaska?

12. What hit show featured four explorers on what was essentially an anthropological expedition, reporting back to their boss, known only as "the Big Giant Head"?

13. Which of these shows was *not* part of ABC's original 1989–90 TGIF lineup?

a) *Perfect Strangers*
b) *Full House*
c) *Dinosaurs*
d) *Family Matters*

14. While only lasting one season, *My So-Called Life* looms large in the psyche of people who grew up in the '90s. Jordan Catalano was Angela's crush, but what was the name of Angela's nerdy neighbor who had a crush on her?

15. What was the name of the Jack Russell terrier who relived stories from famous literature in the eponymous PBS show?

16. In 1992, Johnny Carson retired after 30 years as the host of *The Tonight Show*. A power struggle ensued between two men vying to be the one to take his place, as chronicled in the 1994 book *The Late Shift* by Bill Carter. Who were they?

17. Jon Stewart took over as host of *The Daily Show* in 1999 and became synonymous with the program, but what former SportsCenter anchor was the original host when the show debuted in 1996?

18. The hit series *Charmed* featured Shannon Doherty, Alyssa Milano, and Holly Marie Combs as sisters who discover they are witches when they return to their family home in what U.S. city?

19. On the 1990s sitcom *NewsRadio*, the cast was devastated by beloved comedian Phil Hartman's death in 1998. Rather than recast his role as Bill McNeal, the show had the characters react to McNeal's death in an emotional tribute episode. What fellow *Saturday Night Live* alum stepped into the final season of the show as the news anchor hired to replace him?

20. What newsman was the anchor of NBC's *Nightly News* through the entire 1990s, stepping down in 2004?
a) Brian Williams
b) John Chancellor
c) Tom Brokaw
d) Peter Jennings

21. Cowboy Curtis and his amazing Jheri curl made their final mosey through *Pee-Wee's Playhouse* in November of 1990. What actor, who went on to play an iconic leading role in a 1998 sci-fi blockbuster and its first two sequels, portrayed the lasso-wielding Curtis?

22. The sitcom *Ellen* had a different title when its first season aired in 1994, but it was changed to avoid confusion with another sitcom that premiered later that year. What was it?

Answers on pages 115–116.

Bonus: Feel the Power

Given only their first lines, can you name these power ballads (and identify their artists)? Oh, and here's a bonus toss-up question: do you think more of these songs were written by Diane Warren or by Jim Steinman?

1. Hold on, little girl
   Show me what he's done to you

2. Saying "I love you"
   Is not the words I want to hear from you

3. I don't wanna hear about it anymore
   It's a shame I've got to live without you anymore

4. [REDACTED]
   I'd run right into hell and back
   [REDACTED]
   I'll never lie to you and that's a fact

5. When I look into your eyes
   I can see a love restrained
   But, darlin', when I hold you
   Don't you know I feel the same?

6. There was a time
   When I was so broken-hearted
   Love wasn't much of a friend of mine

7. There were nights when the wind was so cold
   That my body froze in bed
   If I just listened to it right outside the window

8. I'll be your dream, I'll be your wish, I'll be your fantasy
I'll be your hope, I'll be your love, be everything that
you need

9. When your day is long
And the night, the night is yours alone
When you're sure you've had enough of this life
Well, hang on

10. I could stay awake just to hear you breathing
Watch you smile while you are sleeping
While you're far away and dreaming

11. Look into my eyes
You will see
What you mean to me

12. So close, no matter how far
Couldn't be much more from the heart

13. Is it getting better?
Or do you feel the same?
Will it make it easier on you now?
You got someone to blame

14. I follow the Moskva
Down to Gorky Park
Listening to the [REDACTED]

15. Times have changed and times are strange
Here I come, but I ain't the same

16. You and me
We used to be together
Every day together, always

17. [REDACTED]
A new mother cries

18. Well, I just heard the news today
It seems my life is going to change

19. Sometimes I feel like I don't have a partner
Sometimes I feel like my only friend
Is the city I live in, the city of angels
Lonely as I am, together we cry

20. Another turning point, a fork stuck in the road
Time grabs you by the wrist, directs you where to go

 Answers on page 117.

Quiz 18: Play On

1. In the '90s, Barbie's biggest rival was also arguably her smallest. What doll, who was less than an inch tall, came in a playhouse which folded in half and could be carried on your person?

2. Created by Air Force and NASA engineer Lonnie Johnson, what line of plastic toys was introduced in 1991 with the "50" model? (The model number indicated its range in feet.)

3. What toy was the "it" toy of the 1996 Christmas season? It made headlines for being nearly impossible to find, with resellers listing the $30 toy for as much as $1,500.

4. Introduced at the 1993 World Toy Fair, what collectible fad toys of dubious long-term value took their name from the pellets they were stuffed with?

5. What toy introduced to the United States in 1997 has a name that is a portmanteau of the Japanese words for "egg" and "watch"?

6. What cassette voice recorder, which had a speed variation feature that could change a voice's pitch, was originally designed simply as a prop for the film *Home Alone 2: Lost In New York*, but was later released as a real toy by Tiger, who designed the prop?

7. What toy, a sort of bird-hamster thing, arrived from the store speaking its own made-up language, but "learned" English words over time?

8. What was the name of the stuffed animal who came with a set of pens with which you could draw all over them? A quick throw in the wash gave a clean slate for all the future tattoo artists out there. (It was advertised with a parody of Dion's 1961 hit "The Wanderer," in case that helps jog your memory.)

9. What animatronic toy was such a hit as a novelty gift that it appeared in TV shows such as *The Sopranos*, and was reportedly even placed by Queen Elizabeth II upon the grand piano at Balmoral Castle? When it debuted in 1999, it could perform Al Green's "Take Me to the River" as well as Bobby McFerrin's "Don't Worry Be Happy," though its repertoire has expanded since then.

10. What toy, essentially nothing more than a ball on a cord attached to a hoop that loops around one ankle, was originally released in the 1980s but saw a sales boom in the 1990s when it was redesigned in brighter colors, and enhanced with the addition of a counter that recorded your performance?

11. What board game released in 1992 featured players trying to sneak to the refrigerator at night without making noise?

12. As Nickelodeon's star soared in the '90s, they released a number of toys; some were related to their programs, but others were just cool. What item, advertised as "trampolines for your feet," fell mostly into the latter category (though it did appear in some games on "Wild & Crazy Kids" and "GUTS")?

13. Another "just cool" Nickelodeon product was the Time Blaster alarm clock radio, which featured what three-word catchphrase on its box that urged kids to greet the day in a very Nickelodeon-appropriate way?

14. Among the many toys launched by the *Teenage Mutant Ninja Turtles* franchise was a tank-like vehicle which launched plastic versions of what? (Though it seems to me that the heroes in a half shell would have preferred to keep the ammunition for themselves, since it was their favorite food.)

15. You may remember Pogs, which were used to play a game originally played with cardboard caps from milk bottles. The name came from a Hawaiian juice drink called POG, which was not packaged with cardboard caps, but had branded ones made as a promotional item. What did the name "POG" stand for?

16. Released in 1996, the original Bop It! toy had three commands, one of which, of course, was "Bop it!" What were the other two?

Answers on pages 117–118.

Bonus: High-Water Marquees

All these films were among the top-grossing films of the 1990s (not necessarily in order); identify them by the top three billed cast members in each.

1. Leonardo DiCaprio, Kate Winslet, Billy Zane
2. Sam Neill, Laura Dern, Jeff Goldblum
3. Ewan MacGregor, Liam Neeson, Natalie Portman
4. Matthew Broderick, Jeremy Irons, James Earl Jones
5. Will Smith, Bill Pullman, Jeff Goldblum
6. Tom Hanks, Robin Wright, Gary Sinise
7. Bruce Willis, Haley Joel Osment, Toni Collette
8. Jeff Goldblum, Julianne Moore, Pete Postlethwaite
9. Tommy Lee Jones, Will Smith, Linda Fiorentino
10. Bruce Willis, Billy Bob Thornton, Ben Affleck
11. Arnold Schwarzenegger, Linda Hamilton, Edward Furlong
12. Patrick Swayze, Demi Moore, Whoopi Goldberg
13. Scott Weinger, Robin Williams, Linda Larkin
14. Tom Hanks, Tim Allen, Joan Cusack
15. Helen Hunt, Bill Paxton, Cary Elwes
16. Tom Hanks, Matt Damon, Tom Sizemore
17. Robin Williams, Sally Field, Pierce Brosnan
18. Keanu Reeves, Laurence Fishburne, Carrie-Anne Moss
19. Richard Gere, Julia Roberts, Jason Alexander
20. Tom Cruise, Jon Voight, Emmanuelle Béart
21. Tony Goldwyn, Minnie Driver, Brian Blessed

Answers on pages 118–119.

Quiz 19: Innovation Examination

1. While the '60s and '70s belonged to Sweet'n Low, and the '80s and '90s saw Equal moving in on Sweet'n Low's territory, the 2000s definitely belonged to this artificial sweetener brand that was introduced in 1999 and contained sucralose as its main ingredient. What is it?

2. What form did the original Microsoft Office Assistant take when it was introduced in 1997? It would often pop up to help by saying things such as "It looks like you're writing a letter."

3. What company was founded by a British inventor in 1991 to sell his innovative vacuum, and later went on to expand its product lineup to include many other household products, including fans, heaters, air purifiers, hand dryers, and hair dryers?

4. In 1996, Jack Smith and Sabeer Bhatia launched what Internet-based email service? It was one of the first successful services to provide email separately from ISPs, and was acquired by Microsoft in 1997. Although it was incredibly successful, eventually it was fully folded into the Outlook.com email service.

5. What iconic Apple computer was launched in 1998? It created quite a stir for its simple and brightly colored body, ease of use, and lack of floppy disk drive.

6. Years before MP3 players stormed onto the scene, Sony introduced what portable music format in 1992 in hopes of replacing the cassette and competing with the larger CD?

7. While numerous companies had tried to launch personal digital assistants, the first one to really take off was the one released by Palm in 1996. What was the name of that stylish stylus'd PDA?

8. What direct-to-consumer personal computer company decorated their shipping boxes with a cow print?

9. What early ISP distributed so many free trial CDs that at one point half the CDs produced in the world bore the company's logo?
   a) CompuServe
   b) America Online
   c) Prodigy
   d) GEnie

10. What company, whose popular ad spokespuppet was a sock-puppet dog who wore a watch for a collar, became a symbol of the '90s dot-com bust?

11. In 1994, Masahiro Hara invented something to help his employer Denso Wave better track the automotive parts they were producing. The actual invention was inspired by the black and white pieces filling a board of the game Go. What did Hara create, which would become ubiquitous approximately 25 years later?

12. In 1998, Gillette introduced what "revolutionary" line of items which allowed one to shave with less pressure and fewer strokes?

13. Dorm rooms were much stinkier before the 1996 introduction of what air freshener that actually bonds to volatile hydrocarbons, neutralizing many odors instead of just covering them up?

14. Many of the earliest search engines are no longer active (we salute you, AltaVista), but some are still with us, such as Ask.com—although it's lost one word from the name it debuted with in 1996. Its former identity was built around a character who, the idea was, would field naturally worded questions from users. Who was that character, who was officially dropped from the name in 2006?

15. Speaking of search engines, Google changed the game in 1998 with its algorithm that returned more relevant search results. Not unlike Ask.com, for a brief period Google's logo also featured a character that it no longer features today. What was that character?

Answers on pages 119–120.

Bonus: Union Busting

In 1991, the USSR split into 15 individual sovereign nations: Russia and the 14 listed below. Please rotate your book 90° into landscape mode, then match each numbered country with the correct former Soviet Socialist Republic.

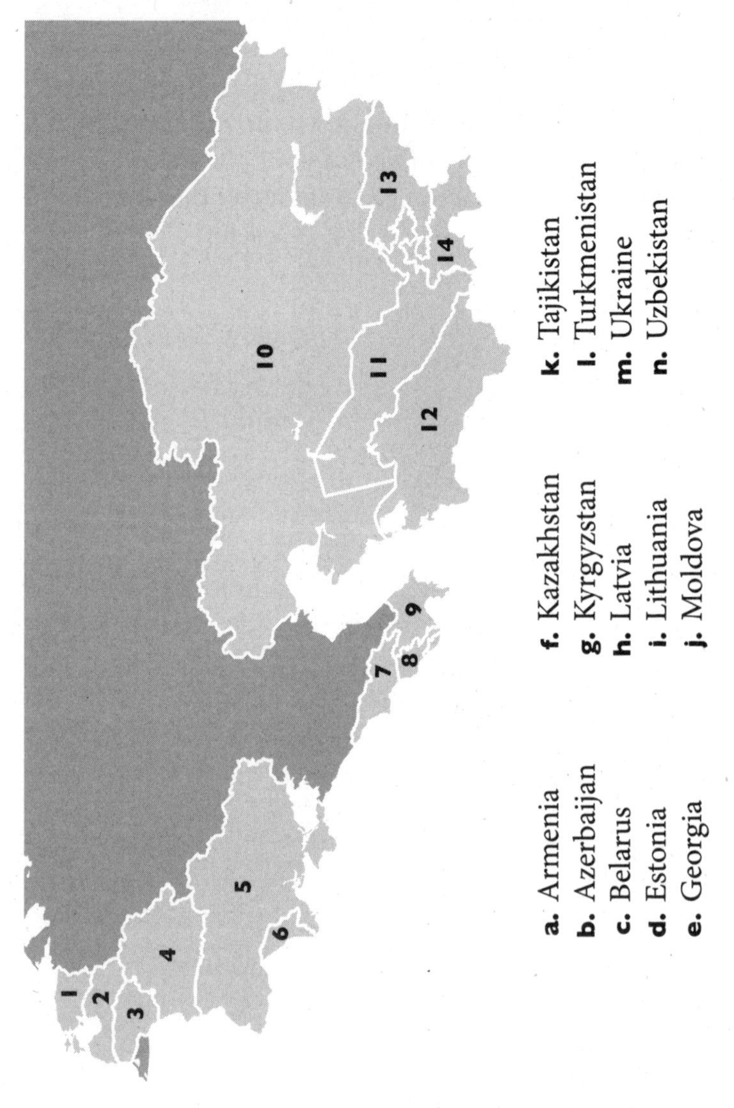

a. Armenia
b. Azerbaijan
c. Belarus
d. Estonia
e. Georgia
f. Kazakhstan
g. Kyrgyzstan
h. Latvia
i. Lithuania
j. Moldova
k. Tajikistan
l. Turkmenistan
m. Ukraine
n. Uzbekistan

Answers on page 120.

Quiz 20: Getting an Earful

1. The rock band Temple of the Dog was originally conceived as a tribute to Andrew Wood, who had been the lead singer of Seattle's Mother Love Bone before passing away at the age of 24 in 1990. Members of Temple of the Dog gained widespread fame as part of the grunge movement with what two bands?

2. Oasis, Blur, Suede, and Pulp are considered the "big four" of what genre of music that was often described as being a reaction against the grunge trend?

3. Another major genre of '90s music took its name from its performers' supposed tendency to look down while performing (probably at their many guitar pedals). What was this genre that was epitomized by bands like My Bloody Valentine, Slowdive, and Lush?

4. What rapper/producer's debut single "Can't Nobody Hold Me Down" spent 28 weeks on the Billboard Hot 100 in 1997—six of those weeks at #1?

5. What rapper born Earl Simmons was a major figure in the Ruff Ryders hip-hop collective, along with fellow Ruff Ryders labelmates like Eve, Jadakiss, and Swizz Beatz?

6. Whose 1992 album *Unplugged*, which was recorded for the TV show *MTV: Unplugged*, became that artist's highest-selling album, and sent one of his songs to the Billboard charts for a second time, over 20 years after its original release? (And what was that song?)

7. After the breakout success of *Nevermind* in 1991, Geffen records rereleased Nirvana's debut album, originally released in 1989 by the indie label Sub Pop. What was its name?

8. Deep Blue Something released what single in 1995 that made them a one-hit wonder? It shares its title with a 1958 novella and a 1961 film based on that novella.

9. 1997's "Flagpole Sitta" was titled after the long-forgotten fad of people sitting on flagpoles for long periods of time (as referenced by Groucho Marx in the film *Animal Crackers*); the lyrics are a commentary on the trendiness of the Seattle music scene. What was this band, who met at the University of Washington and took their name from some graffiti they saw there?

10. When the indie rock band The Housemartins broke up, part of the band went on to form the poppier Beautiful South, but bassist Norman Cook went in a different, more club-oriented direction. He hit #1 in the U.K. in 1990 with "Dub Be Good to Me" as the bandleader of Beats International, but his biggest success began in 1996 when he went solo with a new stage name, under which he popularized the dance music genre known as Big Beat. What was the oxymoronic moniker he adopted?

11. The Flaming Lips had a decade's worth of psychedelic indie rock albums under their belts when they finally broke into the mainstream in 1993 with "She Don't Use Jelly," in which an unnamed girl serves toast with an unusual topping: a product patented in 1872 by Robert Chesebrough, with a name derived from the German word for water and the Greek for oil. At least it's edible; Chesebrough ate a spoonful every day. What is it?

12. The British band Cornershop had a hit in 1997 with a song (and a remix by none other than Norman Cook) that celebrated Indian film culture. The song's title refers to an iconic "playback singer" of Bollywood; what was it?

13. The lead single from Ginuwine's 1996 debut album *Ginuwine ... the Bachelor* was what iconic sex jam?
a) "Too Close"
b) "Pony"
c) "Between the Sheets"
d) "In My Bed"

14. Another musical trend of the 1990s was the nostalgic resurgence of swing and cocktail music. Combustible Edison brought lounge music to indie rock fans with its 1994 debut album on Sub Pop. The swing revival had its first hit single two years later with "Hell," recorded by what band that shared its name with a caramel-and-peanut candy dating back to 1890?

15. In their 1992 music video "Jump," rap duo Kris Kross were seen wearing their fashionable jeans backward (but not inside out, which would have been wiggida-wiggida-wiggida-wack). What brand were those jeans?

16. What comedy duo released their eponymous debut album of prank phone calls in 1993 after Howard Stern boosted their profile by playing their homemade tape recordings on his show? The album topped Billboard's "Heatseekers" chart and went on to go Platinum.

Answers on page 121.

Bonus: Defend Yourself!

Match the *Home Alone* booby traps to the correct locations of Kevin McCallister's house.

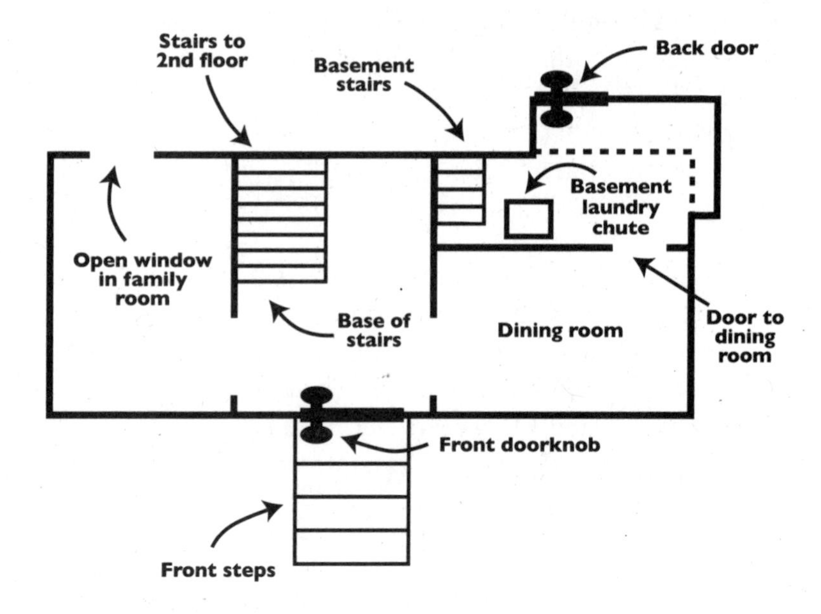

1. Blowtorch
2. Broken Christmas ornaments
3. Electric barbecue starter
4. Falling iron
5. Fan and feathers
6. Plastic wrap covered with glue
7. Ice
8. Micro Machines on floor
9. Swinging paint cans
10. Tar and upturned nail

Answers on page 122.

Quiz 21: On the Books

1. While it may seem like this somewhat traumatic dystopian novel about a society that has taken away pain but also color (and anything else that creates difference) has been around since time immemorial, it was actually first published in 1993! What's the name of this Newbery Medal winner?

2. Book 1 of Philip Pullman's *His Dark Materials* trilogy made its first appearance on shelves back in 1995. In his native U.K., it was entitled *Northern Lights*. What was its North American title, taken from a misunderstood reference to a line from Milton's *Paradise Lost* in the trilogy's working title?

3. Stephen Chbosky's 1999 epistolary novel about adolescents finding themselves in '90s Pittsburgh, which tackled serious issues such as suicide and eating disorders, was entitled *The Perks of Being...* what?

4. Frank McCourt's 1996 memoir *Angela's Ashes* begins with his birth in Brooklyn, New York, but deals primarily with his time living in what country?
   a) Mexico
   b) Ireland
   c) Australia
   d) Italy

5. The *Outlander* time-traveling romance novels set in historical Scotland have become massive hits for Diana Gabaldon, spawning a successful TV series as well. Before becoming a full-time author, she taught environmental science at Arizona State University, and during that time she happened to catch an episode of a TV show about another time traveler, featuring a kilt-wearing Scotsman who inspired the setting of her 1991 debut novel. What was that show?

6. In 1997, Arundhati Roy won the Booker Prize for her debut novel, which follows a pair of fraternal twins as they navigate the casteism and "Love Laws" that governed society in 1960s Kerala, India. What was that book, which became the best-selling novel ever by a non-expatriate Indian author?

7. Gregory Maguire's first novel for adults, released in 1995, was a prequel to a book published almost 100 years earlier, and was subsequently turned into a hit Broadway musical. What was this book that paved the way for the ongoing trend of works that reimagine villains as sympathetic characters?

8. John Berendt's 1994 book *Midnight in the Garden of Good and Evil* was based on real-life events in what southern U.S. city, and featured notable locals such as transgender icon The Lady Chablis?

9. What is the title of Jon Krakauer's 1996 book that attempted to retrace the travels and death in Alaska of Chris McCandless, a.k.a. Alexander Supertramp?

10. David Foster Wallace's postmodern magnum opus of 1996 (which made it onto *Time* magazine's list of the 100 greatest English-language novels published from 1923 to 2005) has what title, taken from a line in *Hamlet*?

11. What 1994 novel won the PEN/Faulkner award for fiction and was adapted to a film in 1999? Its plot revolves around a Japanese-American war veteran accused of murder in the anti-Japanese climate that was pervasive after World War II.

12. Mitch Albom's 1997 memoir, recounting a series of weekly visits to his former sociology professor who was dying from ALS, started out with a modest print run, but eventually saw sales steadily grow until it topped the *New York Times* nonfiction bestseller list in 2000, spending a total of 23 weeks that year as the #1 book. What was the first name of the professor Mitch would visit on Tuesdays?

13. John Gray's best-selling 1992 book of relationship advice suggests that the human race originates from what two locations in outer space? (Nonbinary people are not accounted for.)

14. 1993's *The Shipping News* won both a Pulitzer Prize and a National Book Award. Name its author, who also wrote the 1997 short story "Brokeback Mountain."

15. Novelist Neil Gaiman teamed up with what other author, known for his prolific output of humorous and satirical fantasy novels, to write 1990's *Good Omens*, a comical take on the Apocalypse?

16. In his 1997 Pulitzer-winning nonfiction book, Jared Diamond argued that what three factors (among others) were major forces in the spread and dominance of certain human societies over others?

17. 1990 saw the release of the final Dr. Seuss book to be published in his lifetime, which quickly became a go-to gift for graduates of all ages. Years later, *Star Trek* writer David Gerrold attempted to fund a *Trek*-themed parody of the book (which added the word "Boldly" to its title), but the Seuss estate successfully sued to stop it. What is the title of that Dr. Seuss book?

18. In her 1993 book *The Mole People*, Jennifer Toth described a society of people living in tunnels under what city (although the book's accuracy has been frequently questioned)?

 Answers on pages 122–123.

Bonus: Giving You Goosebumps

Each of the *Goosebumps* titles below is missing a word; can you correctly provide them all by matching up the lists?

1. *Stay Out of the* ___	**a.** Barking
2. *Say* ___ *and Die!*	**b.** Basement
3. *Night of the* ___ *Dummy*	**c.** Breath
4. *The Girl Who Cried* ___	**d.** Camp
5. *Welcome to* ___ *Nightmare*	**e.** Cheese
6. *Piano Lessons Can Be* ___	**f.** Doom
7. *You Can't* ___ *Me!*	**g.** Everyone
8. *Deep* ___	**h.** Hairiest
9. *Go Eat* ___*!*	**i.** Hare
10. ___ *of the Auditorium*	**j.** Invisible
11. *My* ___ *Adventure*	**k.** Lawn
12. *The Cuckoo Clock of* ___	**l.** Legend
13. *It Came From Beneath the* ___*!*	**m.** Living
14. *The* ___ *Ghost*	**n.** Monster
15. *Revenge of the* ___ *Gnomes*	**o.** Murder
16. *How I Got My* ___ *Head*	**p.** Phantom
17. *Bad* ___ *Day*	**q.** Scare
18. *Legend of the Lost* ___	**r.** Shrunken
19. *Vampire* ___	**s.** Sink
20. *Don't Go to* ___*!*	**t.** Sleep
21. *The Blob That Ate* ___	**u.** Trouble
22. *My Best Friend Is* ___	**v.** Worms

Answers on pages 123–124.

Quiz 22: Snack Time

1. Betty Crocker was behind not one, but two iconic lunchbox treats of the early '90s. Both were fruit-flavored; one was a more gimmicky version of Fruit Roll-Ups, the other a gummy candy filled with a juice-like liquid that spurted out when you bit into it ... and both were highly coveted in my elementary school lunchroom. What are their names?

2. Originally invented in the '70s in Taiwan, what candies were introduced to America in 1993 with a name that referenced how explosively sour they were? Being able to withstand the pucker-inducing power conferred instant citrus cred, as I can attest from my experience at sleepaway camp.

3. What kid-targeted drinkable yogurt brand introduced in 1994 initially donated 1.5% of their proceeds to the National Wildlife Federation?

4. What variety of apple, developed at the University of Minnesota, has larger-than-normal cells, making it seem juicier? It hit store shelves for the first time in 1997 and soon became extremely popular; it is now the official state fruit of Minnesota.

5. In 1995, if the commercials were to be believed (and we all know that you can always believe commercials), we could finally stop ordering delivery pizza, thanks to the launch of what gourmet frozen pizza brand?
   a) Totino's
   b) Ellio's
   c) DiGiorno
   d) Amy's

6. What popular snack introduced in 1990 consisted of small packages with cookies and frosting in separate compartments? According to one of their ads featuring an Aussie-accented mascot named Sydney, they tasted real good with "a glass of moo."

7. In the '90s, what frozen snack food ran ads with a jingle that explained "when pizza's on a bagel, you can eat pizza anytime"?

8. Because TV dinners were too "grown up" and Happy Meals meant getting in the car to schlep to McDonald's, in 1990 Conagra launched this Happy Meal–esque frozen dinner brand that was packaged with sticker sets and activity books. What was this product whose original mascots were a penguin and polar bear named B.J. and the Chef, respectively, but who were later replaced by a different penguin with the apt initials K.C.?

9. In 1990, Post introduced a new version of Alpha-Bits featuring marshmallows for which letters?

10. While Wheaties are certainly the breakfast cereal we most associate with pro athletes, the starting quarterback for the Buffalo Bills launched what eponymous frosted cornflake cereal in 1998, with the goal of raising money for charity in honor of his autistic son?

Answers on page 124.

Quiz 23: Animal Kingdom

1. In 1997, *Air Bud* taught us all that there's no rule that says a dog can't play basketball. But what sport did Buddy go on to play in 1998's sequel?

2. For several years, Joey and Chandler had two unusual pets on *Friends*, one young, one fully grown. Over time, the young one grew up, unexpectedly turning out to be male. What were these pets, which caused a bit of a flap when Joey first brought them home from the animal shelter?

3. Speaking of *Friends*, Ross also had an unusual pet for a short time: Marcel the capuchin monkey. Ross ended up donating Marcel to the San Diego Zoo, but after a series of strange circumstances, Marcel ended up as a movie star. Ross was briefly reunited with him while Marcel was filming (with Jean-Claude Van Damme) what fictional sequel subtitled *The Virus Takes Manhattan*?

4. James Cromwell appeared in two '90s films with nearly identical titles; one was a biopic about a baseball player (whose title started with *The*), and the other was about an animal whose name (with no *The*) was the title of the film. What were the two films?

5. What 1998 film featured Garry Shandling as a pigeon, Albert Brooks as a Bengal tiger, Jenna Elfman as an owl, Paul Reubens as a raccoon, Chris Rock as a guinea pig, Ellen DeGeneres as a dog … and, of course, Eddie Murphy in a role played over 30 years earlier by Rex Harrison?

6. Long before the musical *Cats* bombed at the box office in 2019, there was an animated musical about cats … that also bombed in 1997, despite featuring songs by Randy Newman and choreography by Gene Kelly, thanks to a complete lack of marketing due to a studio merger. What was this film, which became the first non-Disney film to win the Annie award for Best Animated Feature?

7. In 1997, a media frenzy was caused by a scientific breakthrough: the first successful cloning of a mammal from a single adult cell—in other words, Dolly the sheep. Who was Dolly named after?

8. Which of the following dinosaurs appear on camera in 1993's *Jurassic Park*?

☐ Brachiosaurus

☐ Triceratops

☐ Velociraptor

☐ Stegosaurus

☐ Ankylosaurus

☐ Gallimimus

☐ Diplodocus

☐ Dimetrodon

☐ Tyrannosaurus rex

☐ Iguanodon

☐ Apatosaurus

☐ Dilophosaurus

9. Match the dogs to the shows:

1. *Dharma & Greg*	**a.** Brian
2. *The Drew Carey Show*	**b.** Buck
3. *Empty Nest*	**c.** Comet
4. *Family Guy*	**d.** Dreyfuss
5. *Frasier*	**e.** Eddie
6. *Full House*	**f.** Murray
7. *Mad About You*	**g.** Santa's Little Helper
8. *Married ... With Children*	**h.** Speedy
9. *The Simpsons*	**i.** Stinky & Nunzio

10. The 1995 Super Bowl featured a commercial with three animals, one of whom was named "Er." What kind of animals were they, what were they advertising, and what were the names of the other two?

Answers on page 125.

Bonus: Where It's At

In what location were each of the these '90s sitcoms based? (Some were in the same city, so you'll use a few of the items in the right-hand list more than once.)

1. *Boy Meets World*
2. *Coach*
3. *The Drew Carey Show*
4. *Dharma & Greg*
5. *Dinosaurs*
6. *Ellen*
7. *Empty Nest*
8. *Family Matters*
9. *Frasier*
10. *Full House*
11. *Hangin' With Mr. Cooper*
12. *Home Improvement*
13. *Living Single*
14. *Mad About You*
15. *Married ... With Children*
16. *Martin*
17. *Murphy Brown*
18. *The Nanny*
19. *Spin City*
20. *Step by Step*
21. *Suddenly Susan*
22. *Wings*

a. Los Angeles, California
b. Oakland, California
c. San Francisco, California
d. Miami. Florida
e. Orlando, Florida
f. Chicago, Illinois
g. Nantucket, Massachusetts
h. Detroit, Michigan
i. New York, New York (Brooklyn)
j. New York, New York (Manhattan)
k. New York, New York (Queens)
l. Cleveland, Ohio
m. Pangaea
n. Philadelphia, Pennsylvania
o. Seattle, Washington
p. Washington, D.C.
q. Port Washington, Wisconsin

Answers on page 126.

Quiz 24: Pixel Perfect

1. What shareware game, released in 1996, took the colored bubbles from the 1980s arcade game Bubble Bobble and replaced them with seven characters? Most people will remember that connecting a group of three or more matching characters will remove them from the screen, but only the truest fans will remember that their names are Geji (light blue), Jake (blue), Midoribe (green), Mildred (gray), Spike (purple), Sunny (yellow), and Zod (red).

2. In 1999, Activision launched a game that would be wildly successful and spawn a number of sequels. In addition to the pro athlete who the game was named for, nine other athletes are playable, including Bucky Lasek and Bob Burnquist. Name that game, which was the third highest-selling game that year.

3. Despite what its title may suggest, this game sequel came out in 1993. It featured a similar concept as the original title released in 1989, but with better graphics, an isometric viewpoint, and a higher emphasis on quality of life. Of course, that quality of life could be affected by various natural disasters, including earthquakes, hurricanes, and monsters. What was this game?

4. According to VGChartz.com, the two top-selling video games in the '90s were both for Nintendo's GameBoy. One involved organizing things and clearing them away, and the other involved collecting things—what are they?

5. While the Nintendo Entertainment System—NES for short—was released in the U.S. in 1985 (and thus will *not* be spoken of in this book!), an aftermarket item released for use with it in 1990 allowed players to unlock a number of cheats or otherwise manipulate gameplay in ways unintended by the developer. What was it called?

6. *The 7th Guest* was a groundbreaking mystery puzzle game. It featured a number of short live-action clips, and its horror milieu scared the crap out of me as a kid. *Myst* was released the same year (and I played it at the same friend's house where I played *The 7th Guest*, though *Myst*'s puzzles went a little over my head at that age). Both games were considered "killer apps" that spurred sales of what computer hardware component?

7. Speaking of *Myst*, it stood out from other games in that it had no time limit, no obvious "bad guy," and no physical violence. Players were transported to an island where they solved environmental puzzles with no instructions in order to uncover a MYSTery. (You see what I did there.) What was the island called?

8. The first MMORPG (short for "massively multiplayer online role-playing game," of course) to employ a 3-D graphics engine was 1995's somewhat obscure *Meridian 59*. By 1999, the technology had improved significantly, as evidenced by the release of the first commercially successful MMORPG to feature 3-D graphics. What was this Dungeons and Dragons–like game, named Game of the Year by Gamespot in 1999?
   a) *World of Warcraft*
   b) *The Elder Scrolls*
   c) *EverQuest*
   d) *Ashen Empires*

9. *Super Mario Bros. 3* was released in North America in 1990 for the NES. The following year, *Super Mario World* was released for the Super Nintendo console (a.k.a. SNES). This game introduced a new character that the player could ride, inspired by one of the game designers' love of horseback riding. What is the name of this friendly dinosaur?

10. What was the name of the accessory, released in 1997 to be used with the Nintendo 64, which caused vibration feedback while playing certain games?

11. The Nomad was a mobile gaming device that allowed people to play games from what home console on the go?

12. What flagship game character was inspired by the color of its parent company's logo, Michael Jackson's shoes, and Bill Clinton's "can-do attitude"?

Answers on pages 126–127.

Bonus: The One Where They Buy a Rhyming Dictionary

The made-up *Friends* episodes in the list below may sound familiar ... because they all rhyme with real *Friends* episodes. For instance, "The One With All the Spreading Messes" is actually "The One With All the Wedding Dresses." How many can you figure out?

1. The One With the Cut
2. The One With the Handy Charts
3. The One With the Warning Laughter
4. The One Where Joe Stuns Eddie
5. The One With the Belly Wish
6. The One With the Best Silk
7. The One With the Looking Glass
8. The One With the Sick Actor
9. The One With the Frail Granny
10. The One With the Trash Rack
11. The One With the All-Groom Glancing
12. The One Where Moss Binds Grout
13. The One With the Wiccan Rocks
14. The One Where Vanna Tries Rice
15. The One With Freebies Buzz-Binned
16. The One With the Three Thieves
17. The One With Hanukkah's Wonder
18. The One Where They Call Vern Dirty

Answers on page 127.

ANSWERS

Quiz 1: ¡Que Linda!

1. Linda Tripp (memorably portrayed on *Saturday Night Live* by John Goodman).
2. Linda Richman.
3. Linda Ronstadt; they won in 1990 for "Don't Know Much" and again in 1991 for "All My Life." (The B-52's lost to them both years with "Love Shack" and "Roam," respectively.)
4. 4 Non Blondes (the chorus doesn't actually say "What's up?" but rather "What's going on?").
5. Linda Hogan, wife of Hulk Hogan.
6. Brandon Lee, *The Crow*.
7. Linda Ellerbee, who continued as anchor/host for the entire original run of the show, through 2015.
8. Paul McCartney. Paul, a vegetarian as well, started the Meat Free Monday campaign in 2009.
9. Jasmine, from *Aladdin*. (Jasmine's singing voice was provided by Lea Salonga, who had just won a Tony in 1991 for her performance in Broadway's *Miss Saigon*.)
10. Sarah Connor
11. Linda Evangelista. Those three models, along with Cindy Crawford and Tatjana Patitz, defined the supermodel era with their January 1990 cover of British Vogue.
12. Lens Express (which was acquired by 1-800 Contacts in 2002).

Quiz 2: The Disney Afternoon

1. *The Jungle Book*.
2. Darkwing Duck.
3. Indiana Jones and Magnum, P.I.
4. c) Max
5. b) *Quack Pack*
6. *Aladdin*, *Timon & Pumbaa*, and *Hercules*.

7. Bonkers.
8. *The Mighty Ducks.*
9. Yummi Gummi was not one of the Gummi Bears.
10. Bronx, Hudson, Lexington, Broadway, and Brooklyn. Keith David, who voiced Goliath, would make another prominent Disney appearance as Dr. Facilier in *The Princess and the Frog*. Among the rest of its cast, *Gargoyles* was notable for its crossover with actors from various incarnations of *Star Trek*; Jonathan Frakes, Marina Sirtis, Michael Dorn, Kate Mulgrew, Nichelle Nichols, Brent Spiner, Avery Brooks, LeVar Burton, and Colm Meaney all voiced characters on the show.

Bonus: *DuckTales* Details

1-b. Bentina Beakley
2-h. Benzino Gassolini
3-f. Farley Foghorn
4-c. Fenton Crackshell
5-k. Fergus McDuck
6-j. Flintheart Glomgold
7-g. Gladstone Gander
8-o. Gloria Swansong
9-m. Goldie O'Gilt
10-i. Gyro Gearloose
11-n. John D. Rockefeather
12-l. Launchpad McQuack
13-r. Ludwig Von Drake
14-a. Ma Beagle
15-e. Magica De Spell
16-t. Oprah Webfeet
17-p. Vacation Van Honk
18-d. Walter Cronduck
19-q. Webby Vanderquack
20-s. Webra Walters

Quiz 3: Bo Knows

1. The California Angels.
2. The Los Angeles Raiders.
3. b) Nike
4. a) Kirk Gibson
   b) Jim Everett
   c) Michael Jordan
   d) John McEnroe
   e) Joan Benoit
   f) Wayne Gretzky
5. Cycling and weights.
6. Bo Diddley was the guitarist, and he said, "Bo, you don't know diddley!"

Quiz 4: 90210

1. c) West Beverly High
2. The Peach Pit.
3. The Peach Pit After Dark.
4. Minnesota.
5. David Silver (played by Brian Austin Green); he ended up graduating a year early so he could follow his friends and his girlfriend Donna to college.
6. Donna Martin (played by Tori Spelling, daughter of Aaron Spelling); Tori actually attended Beverly Hills High School.
7. Andrea.
8. Kelly and David.
9. Tiffani Amber Thiessen, who played Kelly Kapowski on *Saved by the Bell.*
10. Donna.
11. 1-c, 2-e, 3-d, 4-a, 5-b.

Bonus: One and Done

1990: *Cop Rock.*
1991: *Drexell's Class.*
1992: *The Heights.*
1993: *The Adventures of Brisco County, Jr.*
1994: *All-American Girl.*
1995: *Nowhere Man.*
1996: *EZ Streets.*
1997: *George & Leo.*
1998: *Cupid.* Interestingly, a 2009 attempt to reboot this sitcom with Bobby Cannavale and Sarah Paulson also lasted only one season, with seven episodes airing.
1999: *Harsh Realm.* If the title of this show sounds familiar, that might be because it comes from a famous 1992 hoax in which a list of examples of "grunge speak" were reported as fact by *The New York Times,* but had in fact been made up by Megan Jasper (who at the time was a receptionist for the record label Sub Pop; she is now its CEO). "Harsh realm" was said to mean "bummer"; other slang terms in the article included "wack slacks" (old ripped jeans) and "swingin' on the flippity-flop" (hanging out).

Quiz 5: SNICK

1. Ferguson.
2. *The Adventures of Pete & Pete.*
3. *The Secret Life of Alex Mack.* (I had a huge crush on Alex Mack and was bullied in 4th grade for admitting it!)
4. *Are You Afraid of the Dark?*
5. *The Ren and Stimpy Show.*
6. *All That.*
7. Kenan and Kel.
8. *Roundhouse.*
9. *The Mystery Files of Shelby Woo.*
10. Nick at Nite.

Bonus: Alternative Bands

Soundgarden
Candlebox
Melvins
Pearl Jam
Ben Folds Five
Mudhoney
Pixies
Guided by Voices
Sleater-Kinney
Neutral Milk Hotel
Smashing Pumpkins
Elastica
Jane's Addiction
Teenage Fanclub
Veruca Salt

Quiz 6: '90s Potpourri #1

1. Cosmonaut. He was on the space station Mir when the USSR dissolved and was stranded there for nearly twice as long as planned, since the country that sent him up no longer existed!
2. Jack Ryan. Ford played the character in 1992's *Patriot Games* and 1994's *Clear and Present Danger*. Baldwin had previously portrayed Ryan in 1990's *The Hunt for Red October*; Ben Affleck followed in 2002's *The Sum of All Fears*, followed by Chris Pine in 2014's *Jack Ryan: Shadow Recruit*. John Krasinski portrayed the character in the eponymous TV series from 2018 to 2023.
3. Ross Perot.
4. Mikhail Gorbachev (and though there *were* Pizza Huts in Russia, the ad was never aired there).
5. Mark McGwire and Sammy Sosa. McGwire was the first to pass Maris's record, and also completed the season with more home runs (70 to Sosa's 66). Barry Bonds later topped McGwire's record, hitting 73 homers in the 2001 season.

6. The Buffalo Bills.
7. The C-Class, which replaced the 190.
8. Austin Powers, whose nemesis was Dr. Evil.
9. Aurora, Illinois.
10. Jesse Ventura.
11. Albertville, France, hosted the Winter Games, while Barcelona, Spain, hosted the Summer Games.
12. Japan. Perhaps the oddest part of the story is that earlier that day, Bush had played doubles tennis with the U.S. ambassador to Japan against the emperor and crown prince—a game he lost, though it would be more surprising if he had won while suffering from the stomach flu!
13. The Labrador retriever.
14. Pitchfork.
15. Czechoslovakia, which became the Czech Republic (now better known as Czechia) and Slovakia.
16. c) Andrew. Hurricane Andrew caused an estimated 27.3 billion dollars worth of damage (in 1992 dollars).
17. Amy Fisher.
18. a) Edwin Hubble
19. The X Games.
20. Kelly Slater.
21. Tricolore, named for France's three-colored flag. Additionally, the "L" in the Tricolore logo was a stylized cockerel (that is, a rooster), another symbol of France.
22. *Rent.*
23. *Madama Butterfly* (or, as it is commonly referred to, *Madame Butterfly*).
24. *Beauty and the Beast* and *The Lion King*. Disney did have a third successful musical in the '90s—in Germany, where a stage adaptation of their version of *The Hunchback of Notre Dame* opened in June 1999 and ran for 13 years.
25. John Major and Tony Blair.

Bonus: '90s Book-to-Movie Adaptations

1. *The Horse Whisperer.*
2. *American Psycho.*
3. *The Deep End of the Ocean.*
4. *Holes.*
5. *The Girl With the Pearl Earring.*
6. *Bridget Jones's Diary.*
7. *Jurassic Park.*
8. *All the Pretty Horses.*
9. *How Stella Got Her Groove Back.*
10. *The Bridges of Madison County.*
11. *Primary Colors.*
12. *Election.*
13. *Fight Club.*
14. *Trainspotting.*
15. *Angels and Insects.*
16. *Big Fish.*

Quiz 7: Drink Up!

1. Crystal Pepsi. *Saturday Night Live* parodied the product—along with the rest of the clear craze of the '90s—with an ad for "Crystal Gravy."
2. Zima.
3. Surge.
4. The Boston Tea Party.
5. AriZona.
6. Brisk. The ads always featured the clay-lebrities saying, "That's brisk, baby!" While some voices were provided by voice actors (including Joe Piscopo as Frank Sinatra), many were provided by the celebrities themselves, including Sylvester Stallone, George Steinbrenner, James Brown, Coolio, Bruce Willis, Sherman Hemsley, and Isabel Sanford.
7. Orbitz.

8. a) Soda (labeled “cola” in the fridge)
d) O.J.
f) Purple stuff
(There’s also a six-pack of *something* in that refrigerator, but since it wasn’t mentioned, we may never know what it was!)

9. White Russian.

10. Appletini (or Apple Martini). It was originally called Adam’s Apple Martini, after its creator.

11. Cosmopolitan (or cosmo, for short). Although the cosmo as we know it is generally agreed to have been introduced in 1988, a recipe for a very similar cocktail by the same name was published way back in 1934. (Both versions feature triple sec, but the 1934 version used gin instead of vodka, lemon juice instead of lime juice, and raspberry syrup instead of cranberry juice.)

12. Corona Extra.

13. Sierra Mist.

14. Chopin Vodka.

15. Blue Moon.

16. Frappuccino (a combination of “frappe” and “cappuccino”).

17. Bourbon. It was initially founded in 1812 as the Oscar Pepper Distillery, then became the Labrot & Graham Distillery in 1878 until the 1990s rebrand.

18. In chronological order, PepsiCo launched Aquafina in 1994, Dr Pepper launched Dejá Blue in 1996, and Coca-Cola launched Dasani in 1999.

Bonus: Mixed Drinks

1. Surge + Citra (**S**C**UR**IT**GE**RA). Citra was, essentially, a version of Fresca without artificial sweeteners.

2. Sobe + Mistic (**S**MI**O**STI**BE**C).

3. Zima + OK Soda (**Z**O**I**KS**M**O**A**DA). OK Soda attempted to appeal to Gen X with a deliberately disaffected, self-aware ad campaign that included a “manifesto” with lines like “OK Soda may be the preferred drink of other people such as yourself” and “What’s the point of OK? Well, what’s the point of anything?”

4. Tŷ Nant + Josta (TJYONASTNAT). Tŷ Nant was Frasier Crane's preferred brand of bottled water, and its distinctive blue bottles were a frequent sight on the show.
5. Orbitz + Jolt Cola (OJROLBTICOTLZA)
6. Fruitopia + Squeezit (FSRUQUITEOPIEZAIT).
7. Smirnoff Ice + All Sport (SMALIRLNOSPFOFRICTE).
8. Kool-Aid Bursts + Life Savers Soda (KLOIFOLAESIADVERBSUSORDSATS)
9. Fresca Peach Citrus + Hi-C Ecto Cooler (FHIRECSCECAPETACHOCOCITORLEURS)
10. Mountain Dew Sport + Clearly Canadian (MOCULENARTLAINYDECAWSNAPODIRANT)

Quiz 8: Trivia About Nothing ... Except *Seinfeld*

1. Junior Mints.
2. Art Vandelay.
3. *Jerry*.
4. Cosmo.
5. The J. Peterman Catalog.
6. Frogger.
7. Jackie Chiles.
8. Festivus. The holiday of Festivus was originally created by *Seinfeld* writer Dan O'Keefe's father Daniel as a celebration of the anniversary of his first date with his wife, and included a tradition of putting a clock in a bag and nailing the bag to a wall. According to Dan, his father never explained this tradition, saying, "That's not for you to know."
9. H&H Bagels.
10. The Today Sponge.
11. A pirate.
12. Postman.
13. Licking the envelopes for their wedding invitations.
14. Jon Voight.
15. Monk's Café. The exterior is actually Tom's Restaurant on Broadway and 112th Street—which also inspired the song "Tom's Diner" by Suzanne Vega.
16. Larry David, the show's co-creator.

17. Fusilli Jerry and Macaroni Midler (for Bette Midler). He explained to Jerry that he chose fusilli "because you're silly!" (He also claimed to be making a Ravioli George, but sadly, this was never seen.)
18. Kramer, then Elaine.

Bonus: I Wish That I Had Jerry's Girl

These 16 appeared on *Seinfeld* as one of Jerry's short-lived girlfriends: Jennifer Coolidge, Courteney Cox, Kristin Davis, Janeane Garofalo, Jami Gertz, Lauren Graham, Anna Gunn, Teri Hatcher, Catherine Keener, Jane Leeves, Lori Loughlin, Marlee Matlin, Debra Messing, Amanda Peet, Christine Taylor, and Ali Wentworth.

Quiz 9: Get a Clue

1. "Kids in America," originally performed by Kim Wilde.
2. A virgin who can't drive.
3. *Emma.*
4. Paul Rudd.
5. *Scrubs.*
6. Jeep Wrangler.
7. "Rollin' With My Homies."
8. *The Princess Bride.*
9. *Fast Times at Ridgemont High.*
10. Christian.
11. "Well, there goes your social life!"
12. "As if!"
13. Rakuten.
14. b) Stacey Dash, c) Elisa Donovan, f) Donald Faison, and g) Wallace Shawn. Not only did Brittany Murphy not return as Tai, but the character of Tai only appeared in three episodes. She and two other nonreturning cast members (Paul Rudd and Breckin Meyer) did make one-time guest appearances as different characters.

Bonus: To Explore Strange New Prosthetics

1-l. Chakotay, human
2-r. Data, Soong-type android
3-e. Elim Garak, Cardassian
4-g. Guinan, El-Aurian
5-m. Ikat'ika, Jem'Hadar
6-t. Jadzia Dax, Trill
7-q. Kes, Ocampa
8-a. Kira Nerys, Bajoran
9-b. Lwaxana Troi, Betazoid
10-o. Morn, Lurian
11-c. Mot, Bolian
12-i. Naomi Wildman; half human, half Ktarian
13-s. Neelix, Talaxian
14-f. Odo, Changeling
15-h. Quark, Ferengi
16-d. Seven of Nine; Borg, formerly human
17-p. The Caretaker (a.k.a. Banjo Man), Nacene. The Caretaker's natural form was a gelatinous blob of sorts, but it appeared to the *Voyager* crew in the form of an old man playing banjo.
18-k. The Doctor (a.k.a the EMH), hologram. EMH stands for "Emergency Medical Hologram."
19-j. Tuvix; Half Vulcan, half Talaxian (due to a transporter accident involving Tuvok and Neelix)
20-v. Tuvok, Vulcan
21-u. Weyoun, Vorta
22-n. Worf, Klingon

Quiz 10: The Clinton Years

1. c) Arkansas
2. a) Janet Reno
3. The Internet. What Gore actually said was that he had helped create the Internet thanks to his initiatives in Congress (which was true!); he never claimed to have invented the technology.

4. Healthcare.
5. "Don't ask, don't tell."
6. d) Secretary of Labor
7. "It's the economy, stupid." Carville's original phrasing was just "The economy, stupid," but the longer version caught on as an unofficial campaign slogan.
8. Inhale (when he tried marijuana). Bill's actual quote, in response to a question at a candidate forum. was "[W]hen I was in England I experimented with marijuana a time or two, and I didn't like it, and didn't inhale, and never tried it again"; the more succinct "I didn't inhale" is what lived on as a catchphrase.
9. *Black Hawk Down.*
10. Ruth Bader Ginsburg and Stephen Breyer.
11. Goldilocks.
12. Digital Millennium Copyright Act.
13. Sarajevo
14. Slobodan Milošević. He died of a heart attack during the trial, and as a result, the court did not return a verdict.
15. b) Saxophone. He played two songs on the show: "Heartbreak Hotel" and "God Bless the Child."
16. *Contact*. His remarks were edited to make it sound like he was talking about alien messages.
17. Fleetwood Mac's "Don't Stop."
18. d) Jogging. Clinton insisted on jogging outside the grounds of the White House, causing a security headache for the Secret Service, who had to both secure the route and assign agents who could run alongside him while staying alert for threats.

Bonus: Count on Clinton

Clinton won 32 states plus the District of Columbia: Arkansas, California, Colorado, Connecticut, Delaware, D.C., Georgia, Hawaii, Illinois, Iowa, Kentucky, Louisiana, Maine, Maryland, Massachusetts, Michigan, Minnesota, Missouri, Montana, Nevada, New Hampshire, New Jersey, New Mexico, New York, Ohio, Oregon, Pennsylvania, Rhode Island, Tennessee, Vermont, Washington, West Virginia, and Wisconsin.

Quiz 11: Latin Lessons

1. d) "Livin' la Vida Loca"
2. Jennifer Lopez.
3. Marc Anthony.
4. "Bailamos."
5. Carlos Santana.
6. "Smooth."
7. Selena.
8. *General Hospital*; he played singer Miguel Morez. Previously, Ricky Martin had appeared on a Mexican telenovela and had a recurring role on the short-lived sitcom *Getting By*.
9. Christina Aguilera.
10. Bad Bunny.

Quiz 12: Hey Arnold!

1. *Eraser* (1996).
2. *Total Recall* (1990).
3. *True Lies* (1994).
4. *End of Days* (1999).
5. *Junior* (1994).
6. *Kindergarten Cop* (1990).
7. *Last Action Hero* (1993).
8. *Jingle All the Way* (1996).
9. *Batman & Robin* (1997). The scientists in question are, of course, Dr. Victor Fries and Dr. Pamela Isley, better known as Mr. Freeze and Poison Ivy.
10. *Terminator 2: Judgment Day* (1991)

1-b. James Caan played Robert Deguerin in *Eraser*.
2-d. Ronny Cox played Vilos Cohaagen in *Total Recall*.
3-g. Art Malik played Salim Abu Aziz in *True Lies*.
4-a. Gabriel Byrne played a man possessed by Satan in *End of Days*.
5-f. Frank Langella played Noah Banes in *Junior*.

6-j. Richard Tyson played Cullen Crisp Sr. in *Kindergarten Cop*.

7-e. Charles Dance played Mr. Benedict in *Last Action Hero*.

8-i. Sinbad played Myron Larabee in *Jingle All the Way*.

9-c. George Clooney played Bruce Wayne in *Batman & Robin*.

10-h. Robert Patrick played the T-1000 in *Terminator 2: Judgment Day*.

Bonus: Christina Vs. Britney

1. Both were Mouseketeers (as were Justin Timberlake, JC Chasez, Ryan Gosling, and Keri Russell, among others).
2. Britney dated Justin Timberlake.
3. Both performed "Like a Virgin" with Madonna.
4. Both had one #1 hit in 1999 ("Genie in a Bottle" for Christina, and "... Baby One More Time" for Britney. Christina released "What a Girl Wants" in 1999, but it didn't hit #1 until 2000).
5. Christina appeared on the *Mulan* soundtrack (singing the version of "Reflection" that plays over the end credits).
6. Britney has a Broadway musical based on her songs (*Once Upon a One More Time*).
7. Both competed as junior vocalists on *Star Search*.
8. Britney was a judge on the second season of *The X Factor*.
9. Christina was a coach on six of the first ten seasons of *The Voice*.
10. Both did "Carpool Karaoke" with James Corden.
11. Christina won Best New Artist at the 2000 Grammy Awards (Britney was nominated, as were Macy Gray, Kid Rock, and Susan Tedeschi).
12. Christina lived in Japan for multiple years in the early 1980s.
13. Britney appeared as herself on *Glee*.
14. Christina appeared as herself on *Entourage*.
15. Britney was born in McComb, Mississippi.
16. Christina dated back-up dancer Jorge Santos.
17. Britney married back-up dancer Kevin Federline.

18. Both were signed to RCA.
19. Christina had her "Genie in a Bottle" vocals featured alongside the music from the Strokes' "Hard to Explain" in the Freelance Hellraiser mash-up "A Stroke of Genie-Us."
20. Both have been both a host and a musical guest on *Saturday Night Live*.

Quiz 13: Let's Eat

1. Le Pain Quotidien.
2. Jamba Juice.
3. b) Newbury Park. It is currently headquartered in Scottsdale, Arizona.
4. Kenny Rogers Roasters.
5. The Stinking Rose.
6. Arnold Schwarzenegger, Sylvester Stallone, and Bruce Willis.
7. The United Kingdom.
8. Gordon Ramsay.
9. Buca di Beppo (Beppo is a nickname for "Giuseppe," the Italian equivalent of "Joseph").
10. Chipotle.
11. Coyote Ugly Saloon.
12. c) Scottsdale
13. Rainforest Cafe.
14. Wetzel's Pretzels.
15. Wingstop.
16. Einstein Bros. Bagels.
17. Joe's Shanghai.
18. Qdoba.
19. Bubba Gump Shrimp Co.
20. Magnolia Bakery.
21. Robeks.
22. Yard House.
23. Balthazar.
24. Stumptown Coffee Roasters.

Bonus: Disemvoweled '90s Hip-Hop songs

1. "It Was a Good Day," by Ice Cube.
2. "California Love," by 2Pac.
3. "The Humpty Dance," by Digital Underground.
4. "Regulate," by Warren G feat. Nate Dogg.
5. "Nuthin' but a 'G' Thang," by Dr. Dre feat. Snoop Dogg.
6. "Tha Crossroads," by Bone Thugs-N-Harmony.
7. "Make Em' Say Uhh!," by Master P.
8. "Mama Said Knock You Out," by LL Cool J.
9. "My Name Is," by Eminem.
10. "Jump Around," by House of Pain.
11. "Back That Azz Up," by Juvenile.
12. "Can I Kick It?," by A Tribe Called Quest.
13. "Passin' Me By," by the Pharcyde.
14. "Juicy," by the Notorious B.I.G.
15. "Gin and Juice," by Snoop Dogg.
16. "Intergalactic," by Beastie Boys.

Quiz 14: Animaniac Mania

1. d) Yakko, Wakko, Dot
2. In the water tower.
3. "Hello, nurse!" (often said to the studio medic, Heloise Nerz).
4. b) Pigeons
5. Try to take over the world.
6. Orson Welles. (The connection was made even more directly in the *Animaniacs* segment "Yes, Always," which featured Brain re-enacting a famous series of outtakes from Orson Welles voice-overs.)
7. Slappy Squirrel.
8. a) German shepherd
9. Dr. Otto von Scratchansniff.

10. Snowball.
11. a) Good Idea, Bad Idea
12. State capitals, in the song "Wakko's America." (It does have some small flaws, including referring to Jefferson City, Missouri, as "Jefferson.")

Quiz 15: '90s Potpourri #2

1. d) Yitzhak Rabin
2. NAFTA (North American Free Trade Agreement).
3. Newt Gingrich.
4. Dan Quayle.
5. The Hale-Bopp comet.
6. Waco.
7. Inline skates. During the journey, a drunk driver in Colorado struck him and broke both of his legs, which required nine months of recovery—but he completed his route afterward.
8. "Friday I'm in Love." Interestingly, the song, which was composed in D major, was accidentally recorded with the multi-track recorder's vari-speed function switched on, leading to the released version of the song being sped up by a quarter tone—so, technically, it's in the key of D semi-sharp major.
9. White Diamonds.
10. The George Foreman Grill. In Asian markets, it was sold as the Jackie Chan Grill!
11. The Aeron.
12. Netflix.
13. "The wrong kind of snow." The phrase has come to signify any similarly inadequate excuse.
14. "Can we all get along?"
15. Beef.

Bonus: Celebrity Couples

1. Brad Pitt and Gwyneth Paltrow.
2. Kate Moss and Johnny Depp.
3. Matt Damon and Minnie Driver.
4. Nicole Kidman and Tom Cruise.
5. Bruce Willis and Demi Moore.
6. Richard Gere and Cindy Crawford.
7. Pamela Anderson and Tommy Lee.
8. Julia Roberts and Lyle Lovett.
9. Posh Spice (now Victoria Beckham) and David Beckham.

Quiz 16: Screen Test

1. 50 mph.
2. A cruise ship. (It was hijacked and programmed to crash into an oil tanker.)
3. John Travolta and Nicolas Cage.
4. *Cliffhanger*. The scene was parodied in the opening of the 1995 film *Ace Ventura: When Nature Calls* with Jim Carrey's character failing to rescue a stranded raccoon.
5. *Bill and Ted's Bogus Journey*.
6. *Star Wars Episode I: The Phantom Menace*.
7. *Son in Law*.
8. c) The Rockford Peaches. The Belles, Blue Sox, and Comets were teams they competed against.
9. *Rounders*.
10. *Eyes Wide Shut*.
11. Puppetry (specifically, marionettes).
12. *Toy Story*.
13. *Barb Wire*.
14. *Four Weddings and a Funeral*.
15. a) Pierce Brosnan
16. *My Cousin Vinny*.
17. *Romeo and Juliet*; the two lovers were played by Joseph Fiennes (brother of Ralph) and Gwyneth Paltrow.
18. e) Sting. Elton and Elvis played themselves.
19. Census taker.

Bonus: Oh, Boy Bands

98 Degrees:
Nick Lachey
Jeff Timmons
Justin Jeffre
Drew Lachey

Backstreet Boys:
Nick Carter
AJ McLean
Brian Littrell
Howie Dorough
Kevin Richardson

Boyz II Men:
Nathan Morris
Wanyá Morris
Shawn Stockman
Michael McCary

NSYNC:
Justin Timberlake
JC Chasez
Joey Fatone
Chris Kirkpatrick
Lance Bass

Quiz 17: (Small) Screen Test

1. *Law & Order.*
2. *The Fresh Prince of Bel-Air*, starring Will Smith, who performed and co-wrote the rap with his collaborator DJ Jazzy Jeff; Quincy Jones composed the underlying music. (The official title of that theme song, incidentally, is "Yo Home to Bel-Air.")

3. *Frasier*; star Kelsey Grammer performed the theme. The title "Tossed Salad and Scrambled Eggs" was meant to refer to the mixed-up people who called in to Frasier's radio show (both tossed salad and scrambled eggs being things that are mixed up).
4. *Baywatch*; the first season was the only one to air on network television. After being canceled by NBC, the following seasons aired in first-run syndication.
5. Rockapella. That theme song was co-written by band member Sean Altman and David Yazbek, who would go on to compose many Broadway musicals, including the Tony-winning Best Musical *The Band's Visit*.
6. Jerry Springer.
7. Ricki Lake.
8. *South Park*.
9. d) Maggie
10. Red, black, yellow, pink, and blue
11. *Northern Exposure*.
12. *Third Rock From the Sun*. The Big Giant Head was portrayed by William Shatner.
13. c) *Dinosaurs*. It joined in the second season of the ABC TGIF block.
14. Brian Krakow.
15. Wishbone.
16. David Letterman and Jay Leno.
17. Craig Kilborn.
18. San Francisco.
19. Jon Lovitz.
20. c) Tom Brokaw. John Chancellor was the anchor who preceded him; Brian Williams followed him; and Peter Jennings hosted the rival program *ABC World News Tonight*.
21. Laurence Fishburne (credited at the time as Larry Fishburne).
22. *These Friends of Mine*, deemed too similar to *Friends*.

Bonus: Feel the Power

1. "To Be With You" by Mr. Big.
2. "More Than Words" by Extreme.
3. "High Enough" by Damn Yankees.
4. "I'd Do Anything for Love (But I Won't Do That)" by Meatloaf.
5. "November Rain" by Guns N' Roses.
6. "Cryin'" by Aerosmith.
7. "It's All Coming Back to Me Now" by Céline Dion.
8. "Truly Madly Deeply" by Savage Garden.
9. "Everybody Hurts" by R.E.M.
10. "I Don't Want to Miss a Thing" by Aerosmith.
11. "(Everything I Do) I Do It for You" by Bryan Adams.
12. "Nothing Else Matters" by Metallica.
13. "One" by U2.
14. "Wind of Change" by Scorpions.
15. "Mama, I'm Comin' Home" by Ozzy Osbourne.
16. "Don't Speak" by No Doubt.
17. "Lightning Crashes" by Live.
18. "With Arms Wide Open" by Creed.
19. "Under the Bridge" by Red Hot Chili Peppers.
20. "Good Riddance (Time of Your Life)" by Green Day.

Jim Steinman wrote two of the above songs (#4 and #7), and Diane Warren wrote only one of them (#10).

Quiz 18: Play On

1. Polly Pocket.
2. Super Soaker.
3. Tickle Me Elmo.
4. Beanie Babies.

5. Tamagotchi, from tamago (egg) + uotchi (watch). The virtual pets may not be as ubiquitous today as they once were, but they're still around; Bandai even released a Tamagotchi smart watch in 2021.
6. Talkboy. Kevin McCallister uses the voice-changing effects to trick and mislead adults in the film.
7. Furby; its language is known as Furbish. Despite what their marketing implied, Furby toys didn't actually learn English by interacting with their users; they were simply programmed to gradually introduce English words into their speech.
8. Doodle Bear.
9. Big Mouth Billy Bass.
10. Skip-It. To play with it, you jogged in place, spinning the hoop on one ankle and jumping over the cord with the other.
11. Don't Wake Daddy. (I may need to buy this one to help instill the sentiment in my kids!)
12. Moon Shoes.
13. "Rise & Slime!"
14. Pizzas. (The toy was called the Pizza Thrower, and was later repackaged as the Sewer Lid Launcher, among other tie-ins.)
15. Pineapple, orange, guava.
16. "Twist it!" and "Pull it!"

Bonus: High-Water Marquees

1. *Titanic.*
2. *Jurassic Park.*
3. *Star Wars: Episode I—The Phantom Menace.*
4. *The Lion King.*
5. *Independence Day.*
6. *Forrest Gump.*
7. *The Sixth Sense.*
8. *The Lost World: Jurassic Park.*
9. *Men in Black.*
10. *Armageddon.*
11. *Terminator 2: Judgment Day.*
12. *Ghost.*

13. *Aladdin.*
14. *Toy Story 2.*
15. *Twister.*
16. *Saving Private Ryan.*
17. *Mrs. Doubtfire.*
18. *The Matrix.*
19. *Pretty Woman.*
20. *Mission: Impossible.*
21. *Tarzan.*

Quiz 19: Innovation Examination

1. Splenda. On *The Office*, Michael Scott's preferred cocktail was scotch and Splenda: "Tastes like Splenda, gets you drunk like scotch."
2. An animated paper clip named Clippit (or, as it was more commonly known, Clippy). After 10 years, it was finally discontinued as Microsoft released the Clippy-free Office 2007 for Windows/Office 2008 for Mac.
3. Dyson.
4. Hotmail.
5. iMac. The original five colors were red, orange, green, blue, and purple—or, rather, strawberry, tangerine, lime, blueberry, and grape.
6. MiniDisc.
7. PalmPilot.
8. Gateway (then called Gateway 2000).
9. b) America Online
10. Pets.com. The iconic puppet was voiced by comedian Michael Ian Black, and made one appearance as a balloon in the Macy's Thanksgiving Day Parade in 1999.
11. QR codes.
12. Mach 3, the first triple-blade razor cartridge. Gillette was so concerned about secrecy that prior to launch they erected temporary walls in the factory so employees who weren't working on the product wouldn't see.
13. Febreze.

14. Jeeves, named after Bertie Wooster's valet in the stories by P.G. Wodehouse. Jeeves also appeared in the Macy's Thanksgiving Day Parade, first as a statue on a float in 1999, then as a balloon in 2000–02 and 2004.

15. An exclamation point.

Bonus: Union Busting

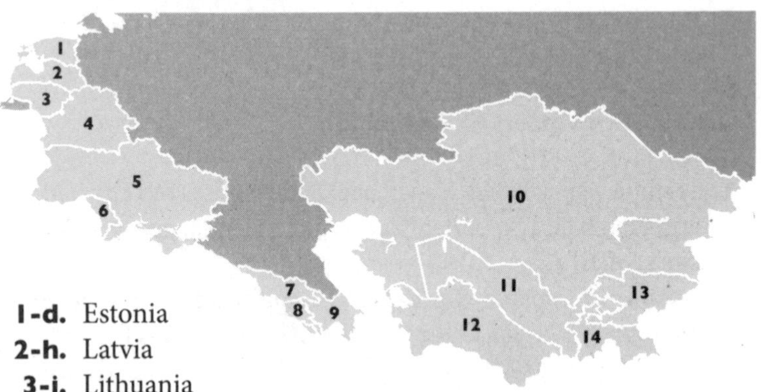

1-d. Estonia
2-h. Latvia
3-i. Lithuania
4-c. Belarus
5-m. Ukraine
6-j. Moldova
7-e. Georgia
8-a. Armenia
9-b. Azerbaijan
10-f. Kazakhstan
11-n. Uzbekistan
12-l. Turkmenistan
13-g. Kyrgyzstan
14-k. Tajikistan

Incidentally, in case you were wondering, that little dark gray area to the west of Lithuania is actually part of Russia; it's known as the Kaliningrad Oblast.

Quiz 20: Getting an Earful

1. Pearl Jam and Soundgarden. The band members included Chris Cornell of Soundgarden; Eddie Vedder, Stone Gossard, Jeff Ament, and Mike McCready of Pearl Jam—and Matt Cameron, who played with both bands!
2. Britpop.
3. Shoegaze.
4. Puff Daddy (a.k.a. Diddy, a.k.a. Sean Combs).
5. DMX. His 1998 hit "Ruff Ryders Anthem" is a reference to this.
6. Eric Clapton, who had reached #10 with the original release of "Layla" by Derek and the Dominos, and made it to #12 with his acoustic version. The other single from the album, "Tears In Heaven," peaked at #2 behind Vanessa Williams's "Save the Best for Last."
7. *Bleach.*
8. "Breakfast at Tiffany's." The song was actually inspired by lead singer Todd Pipes watching part of the film *Roman Holiday*, but he decided the other Audrey Hepburn movie sounded better.
9. Harvey Danger.
10. Fatboy Slim.
11. Vaseline.
12. "Brimful of Asha." A playback singer, in Bollywood, is someone who records vocals that are then lip-synced in the movie; the Asha referenced in the song is Asha Bhosle, who is one of the most renowned playback singers and has recorded over 12,000 songs.
13. b) Pony
14. Squirrel Nut Zippers.
15. Marithé + François Girbaud. The company led the charge on the process of industrialized stone washing
16. The Jerky Boys.

Bonus: Defend Yourself!

1. Back door.
2. Open window in family room.
3. Front doorknob. The electric barbecue starter looped over the knob to heat it up.
4. Basement laundry chute. Marv (Daniel Stern) triggered this by tugging on a string he thought would turn on the ceiling light, but was actually attached to an iron at the top of the chute.
5. Dining room.
6. Door to dining room. After Harry (Joe Pesci) walked through the door into the glue-covered plastic wrap, the fan in the room, triggered by a tripwire, blew feathers at him.
7. Front steps.
8. Base of stairs.
9. Stairs to 2nd floor.
10. Basement stairs.

Quiz 21: On the Books

1. *The Giver.*
2. *The Golden Compass.* The working title of the trilogy before publication had been *The Golden Compasses*, referring to a line from *Paradise Lost* in which Milton poetically describes God delineating the boundary of the universe. The U.S. publisher assumed this was a reference to the main character's "alethiometer" (a mystical device that could, if used correctly, truthfully answer questions) and became attached to it.
3. *The Perks of Being a Wallflower.*
4. b) Ireland
5. *Doctor Who.* The character that caught her fancy (in the episode "The War Games") was Jamie, a companion of Patrick Troughton's Doctor.

6. *The God of Small Things.*
7. *Wicked: The Life and Times of the Wicked Witch of the West.*
8. Savannah, Georgia.
9. *Into the Wild.*
10. *Infinite Jest.* The phrase is heard when Hamlet is musing upon the skull of Yorick, the jester: "Alas, poor Yorick! I knew him, Horatio: a fellow of infinite jest, of most excellent fancy."
11. *Snow Falling on Cedars.*
12. Morrie.
13. Mars and Venus (in the book *Men Are From Mars, Women Are From Venus*).
14. Annie Proulx.
15. Terry Pratchett.
16. *Guns, Germs, and Steel.*
17. *Oh, the Places You'll Go!* (The attempted parody, of course, was *Oh, the Places You'll Boldly Go!*)
18. New York.

Bonus: Giving You Goosebumps

1-b. *Stay Out of the Basement*
2-e. *Say Cheese and Die!*
3-m. *Night of the Living Dummy*
4-n. *The Girl Who Cried Monster*
5-d. *Welcome to Camp Nightmare*
6-o. *Piano Lessons Can Be Murder*
7-q. *You Can't Scare Me!*
8-u. *Deep Trouble*
9-v. *Go Eat Worms!*
10-p. *Phantom of the Auditorium*
11-h. *My Hairiest Adventure*
12-f. *The Cuckoo Clock of Doom*
13-s. *It Came From Beneath the Sink!*
14-a. *The Barking Ghost*
15-k. *Revenge of the Lawn Gnomes*

16-r. *How I Got My Shrunken Head*
17-i. *Bad Hare Day*
18-l. *Legend of the Lost Legend*
19-c. *Vampire Breath*
20-t. *Don't Go to Sleep!*
21-g. *The Blob That Ate Everyone*
22-j. *My Best Friend Is Invisible*

Quiz 22: Snack Time

1. Fruit by the Foot, Gushers (a.k.a Fruit Gushers). Not a company to rest on its laurels, Betty Crocker followed those up with another innovative fruit snack, Fruit String Thing, whose packages contained a long string-shaped fruit chew stuck to a white backing card, laid out to create designs such as a pair of sunglasses or a rocket ship.
2. Warheads.
3. Danimals. (You may be able to tell from that name that it was made by Dannon.)
4. The Honeycrisp. During its early development in the '70s, it was nearly discarded because the program's goal was to breed winter-hardy apples, which the Honeycrisp was not.
5. c) DiGiorno, known for the slogan "It's not delivery, it's DiGiorno." Though now I wonder what happens if you Instacart a DiGiorno pizza....
6. Dunkaroos.
7. Bagel Bites. Fun fact: This was the basis of my college application essay! (Basically, it examined the ramifications of Bagel Bites being defined as "pizza on a bagel," which implies that "pizza" = "sauce and cheese." But sauceless pizza and cheeseless pizza both exist, so ... is pizza anything?)
8. Kid Cuisine.
9. The vowels: pink A's, yellow E's, purple I's, orange O's, green U's, and, eventually, blue Y's.
10. Flutie Flakes, launched by Doug Flutie.

Quiz 23: Animal Kingdom

1. Football, in *Air Bud: Golden Receiver.*
2. A chick and a duck (later a rooster and a duck).
3. *Outbreak 2.*
4. 1992's *The Babe* (starring John Goodman as Babe Ruth) and 1995's *Babe* (starring over 40 piglets as the titular sheep-herding pig).
5. *Dr. Dolittle.*
6. *Cats Don't Dance.*
7. Dolly Parton, for the rather juvenile reason that the cloned cell came from a mammary gland. In a 2014 interview, Dolly remarked, "I never met [Dolly the sheep] but I always said there's no such thing as baa-a-d publicity."
8. Six of the dinosaurs appeared in *Jurassic Park*: Brachiosaurus, Triceratops, Velociraptor, Gallimimus, Tyrannosaurus rex, and Dilophosaurus.
9. **1-i.** *Dharma & Greg*, Stinky & Nunzio
   2-h. *The Drew Carey Show*, Speedy
   3-d. *Empty Nest*, Dreyfuss
   4-a. *Family Guy*, Brian
   5-e. *Frasier*, Eddie
   6-c. *Full House*, Comet
   7-f. *Mad About You*, Murray
   8-b. *Married ... With Children*, Buck
   9-g. *The Simpsons*, Santa's Little Helper
10. They were frogs advertising Budweiser; the other two were named "Bud" and "Weis." (I had a parody shirt on which the three frogs said "Butt," "Why," and "Per"—peak comedy, I know.)

Bonus: Where It's At

1-n. *Boy Meets World;* Philadelphia, Pennsylvania
2-e. *Coach*; Orlando, Florida
3-l. *The Drew Carey Show*; Cleveland, Ohio
4-c. *Dharma & Greg*; San Francisco, California
5-m. *Dinosaurs*; Pangaea
6-a. *Ellen*; Los Angeles, California
7-d. *Empty Nest*; Miami. Florida
8-f. *Family Matters*; Chicago, Illinois
9-o. *Frasier*; Seattle, Washington
10-c. *Full House*; San Francisco, California
11-b. *Hangin' With Mr. Cooper*; Oakland, California
12-h. *Home Improvement*; Detroit, Michigan
13-i. *Living Single*; New York, New York (Brooklyn)
14-j. *Mad About You*; New York, New York (Manhattan)
15-f. *Married ... With Children*; Chicago, Illinois
16-h. *Martin*; Detroit, Michigan
17-p. *Murphy Brown*; Washington, D.C.
18-k. *The Nanny*; New York, New York (Queens)
19-j. *Spin City*; New York, New York (Manhattan)
20-q. *Step by Step*; Port Washington, Wisconsin
21-c. *Suddenly Susan*; San Francisco, California
22-g. *Wings*; Nantucket, Massachusetts

Quiz 24: Pixel Perfect

1. *Snood.* While many may fondly recall it as a classic timewaster, no less a luminary than Apple co-founder Steve Wozniak said it was one of his favorite games.
2. *Tony Hawk's Pro Skater.* Due to his royalty deal, Hawk allegedly earned 10 times what Activision initially offered him in the deal.
3. *SimCity 2000.*

4. *Tetris* and *Pokémon Red/Blue*. The latter was originally released in Japan as *Pocket Monsters Red/Green*; differently colored special editions of both versions followed later.
5. Game Genie.
6. The CD-ROM drive.
7. Myst was the name of the island. (I think I'm allowed one trick question!)
8. c) *EverQuest*. This was the only MMORPG I ever played and I *loved* it. I used to lose entire nights playing it with my friends, fueled by many Dr Peppers.
9. Yoshi.
10. The Rumble Pak.
11. Sega Genesis.
12. Sonic the Hedgehog.

Bonus: The One Where They Buy a Rhyming Dictionary

1. The One With the Butt
2. The One With the Candy Hearts
3. The One With the Morning After
4. The One Where No One's Ready
5. The One With the Jellyfish
6. The One With the Breast Milk
7. The One With the Cooking Class
8. The One With the Ick Factor
9. The One With the Male Nanny
10. The One With the Flashback
11. The One With the Ballroom Dancing
12. The One Where Ross Finds Out
13. The One With the Chicken Pox
14. The One Where Nana Dies Twice
15. The One With Phoebe's Husband
16. The One With the Tea Leaves
17. The One With Monica's Thunder
18. The One Where They All Turn Thirty

About the Author

Buzzy Cohen is a music supervisor originally from New Jersey who now resides in Los Angeles. He came to public attention during his 9-game winning streak on *Jeopardy!* in 2016, and cemented himself as a fan favorite by winning the 2017 Tournament of Champions. In 2021, he served as a guest host for the Tournament of Champions.

Dubbed "Mr. Personality" by Alex Trebek, Buzzy is known for his singular style and irreverent sense of humor as much as his impressive brains. He joined ABC's *The Chase* in Season 3 where he's known as "The Stunner," and also hosts the podcasts *This Is Jeopardy!* and *Inside Jeopardy!*

Buzzy's passion for learning and challenging himself has led him to some surprising endeavors, including winning a national deadlift championship and learning how to tap dance. These experiences inspired his book *Get Ready: A Champion's Guide to Preparing for the Moments That Matter*, which was released as an Audible Original in June 2020. When he's not selecting music for ads, winning trivia competitions, lifting, playing Brazilian-style guitar, tap dancing, collecting classic cars, cycling, or surfing, Buzzy spends all his time with his wife and two children.

Acknowledgments

I'd like to thank so many people for making this happen: Nicole Tourtelot at The Gernet Company for always having my back; my editor, Francis Heaney, for an unfair amount of help and amazing ideas for quizzes and puzzles; John deBary for circuitously making this happen; Kasey Esser for talking Arnold with me; my sister Lindsay for making sure I was hip during the '90s; my folks for nurturing my love of trivia and pop culture; my kids for reminding me that everything from the '90s is very old (including me); and, most importantly, my wife for giving me lots of material and being the first sounding board for the quizzes in this book.